Wendi Arant, MLS
Candace R. Benefiel, MA, MLIS
Editors

The Image and Role of the Librarian

The Image and Role of the Librarian has been co-published simultaneously as *The Reference Librarian*, Number 78 2002.

Pre-publication REVIEWS, COMMENTARIES, EVALUATIONS . . .

"EXTREMELY VALUABLE. . . . COMPREHENSIVE . . . balanced, thorough, scholarly, yet extremely readable and often entertaining. . . . The combined bibliographies provide a comprehensive reference source for some of the most important research available on the subject. From Harvard's John Winthrop, America's first librarian, named in 1672, to Rupert Giles, the fictional librarian at Sunnyvale High on the television program 'Buffy the Vampire Slayer,' this book offers a treasure-trove of library history that SHOULD SERVE AS A PRIMARY TEXT IN AMERICA'S GRADUATE LIBRARY SCHOOLS."

Bruce E. Massis, MLS, MA
Author
The Practical Library Manager
Associate Director
Southeast Florida Library Information Network (SEFLIN)

The Haworth Information Press
An Imprint of The Haworth Press, Inc.

The Image and Role
of the Librarian

The Image and Role of the Librarian has been co-published simultaneously as *The Reference Librarian*, Number 78 2002.

The Reference Librarian Monographic "Separates"

Below is a list of "separates," which in serials librarianship means a special issue simultaneously published as a special journal issue or double-issue *and* as a "separate" hardbound monograph. (This is a format which we also call a "DocuSerial.")

"Separates" are published because specialized libraries or professionals may wish to purchase a specific thematic issue by itself in a format which can be separately cataloged and shelved, as opposed to purchasing the journal on an on-going basis. Faculty members may also more easily consider a "separate" for classroom adoption.

"Separates" are carefully classified separately with the major book jobbers so that the journal tie-in can be noted on new book order slips to avoid duplicate purchasing.

You may wish to visit Haworth's Website at . . .

http://www.HaworthPress.com

. . . to search our online catalog for complete tables of contents of these separates and related publications.

You may also call 1-800-HAWORTH (outside US/Canada: 607-722-5857), or Fax 1-800-895-0582 (outside US/Canada: 607-771-0012), or e-mail at:

docdelivery@haworthpress.com

The Image and Role of the Librarian, edited by Wendi Arant, MLS, and Candace R. Benefiel, MA, MLIS (No. 78, 2002). *A unique and insightful examination of how librarians are perceived–and how they perceive themselves.*

Distance Learning: Information Access and Services for Virtual Users, edited by Hemalata Iyer, PhD (No. 77, 2002). *Addresses the challenge of providing Web-based library instructional materials in a time of ever-changing technologies.*

Helping the Difficult Library Patron: New Approaches to Examining and Resolving a Long-Standing and Ongoing Problem, edited by Kwasi Sarkodie-Mensah, PhD (No. 75/76, 2002). *"Finally! A book that fills in the information cracks not covered in library school about the ubiquitous problem patron. Required reading for public service librarians." (Cheryl LaGuardia, MLS, Head of Instructional Services for the Harvard College Library, Cambridge, Massachusetts)*

Evolution in Reference and Information Services: The Impact of the Internet, edited by Di Su, MLS (No. 74, 2001). *Helps you make the most of the changes brought to the profession by the Internet.*

Doing the Work of Reference: Practical Tips for Excelling as a Reference Librarian, edited by Celia Hales Mabry, PhD (No. 72 and 73, 2001). *"An excellent handbook for reference librarians who wish to move from novice to expert. Topical coverage is extensive and is presented by the best guides possible: practicing reference librarians." (Rebecca Watson-Boone, PhD, President, Center for the Study of Information Professionals, Inc.)*

New Technologies and Reference Services, edited by Bill Katz, PhD (No. 71, 2000). *This important book explores developing trends in publishing, information literacy in the reference environment, reference provision in adult basic and community education, searching sessions, outreach programs, locating moving image materials for multimedia development, and much more.*

Reference Services for the Adult Learner: Challenging Issues for the Traditional and Technological Era, edited by Kwasi Sarkodie-Mensah, PhD (No. 69/70, 2000). *Containing research from librarians and adult learners from the United States, Canada, and Australia, this comprehensive guide offers you strategies for teaching adult patrons that will enable them to properly use and easily locate all of the materials in your library.*

Library Outreach, Partnerships, and Distance Education: Reference Librarians at the Gateway, edited by Wendi Arant and Pixey Anne Mosley (No. 67/68, 1999). *Focuses on community outreach in libraries toward a broader public by extending services based on recent developments in information technology.*

From Past-Present to Future-Perfect: A Tribute to Charles A. Bunge and the Challenges of Contemporary Reference Service, edited by Chris D. Ferguson, PhD (No. 66, 1999). *Explore reprints of selected articles by Charles Bunge, bibliographies of his published work, and original articles that draw on Bunge's values and ideas in assessing the present and shaping the future of reference service.*

Reference Services and Media, edited by Martha Merrill, PhD (No. 65, 1999). *Gives you valuable information about various aspects of reference services and media, including changes, planning issues, and the use and impact of new technologies.*

Coming of Age in Reference Services: A Case History of the Washington State University Libraries, edited by Christy Zlatos, MSLS (No. 64, 1999). *A celebration of the perseverance, ingenuity, and talent of the librarians who have served, past and present, at the Holland Library reference desk.*

Document Delivery Services: Contrasting Views, edited by Robin Kinder, MLS (No. 63, 1999). *Reviews the planning and process of implementing document delivery in four university libraries–Miami University, University of Colorado at Denver, University of Montana at Missoula, and Purdue University Libraries.*

The Holocaust: Memories, Research, Reference, edited by Robert Hauptman, PhD, and Susan Hubbs Motin (No. 61/62, 1998). *"A wonderful resource for reference librarians, students, and teachers . . . on how to present this painful, historical event." (Ephraim Kaye, PhD, The International School for Holocaust Studies, Yad Vashem, Jerusalem)*

Electronic Resources: Use and User Behavior, edited by Hemalata Iyer, PhD (No. 60, 1998). *Covers electronic resources and their use in libraries, with emphasis on the Internet and the Geographic Information Systems (GIS).*

Philosophies of Reference Service, edited by Celia Hales Mabry (No. 59, 1997). *"Recommended reading for any manager responsible for managing reference services and hiring reference librarians in any type of library." (Charles R. Anderson, MLS, Associate Director for Public Services, King County Library System, Bellevue, Washington)*

Business Reference Services and Sources: How End Users and Librarians Work Together, edited by Katherine M. Shelfer (No. 58, 1997). *"This is an important collection of papers suitable for all business librarians. . . . Highly recommended!" (Lucy Heckman, MLS, MBA, Business and Economics Reference Librarian, St. John's University, Jamaica, New York)*

Reference Sources on the Internet: Off the Shelf and onto the Web, edited by Karen R. Diaz (No. 57, 1997). *Surf off the library shelves and onto the Internet and cut your research time in half!*

Reference Services for Archives and Manuscripts, edited by Laura B. Cohen (No. 56, 1997). *"Features stimulating and interesting essays on security in archives, ethics in the archival profession, and electronic records." ("The Year's Best Professional Reading" (1998), Library Journal)*

Career Planning and Job Searching in the Information Age, edited by Elizabeth A. Lorenzen, MLS (No. 55, 1996). *"Offers stimulating background for dealing with the issues of technology and service. . . . A reference tool to be looked at often." (The One-Person Library)*

The Roles of Reference Librarians: Today and Tomorrow, edited by Kathleen Low, MLS (No. 54, 1996). *"A great asset to all reference collections. . . . Presents important, valuable information for reference librarians as well as other library users." (Library Times International)*

Reference Services for the Unserved, edited by Fay Zipkowitz, MSLS, DA (No. 53, 1996). *"A useful tool in developing strategies to provide services to all patrons." (Science Books & Films)*

Library Instruction Revisited: Bibliographic Instruction Comes of Age, edited by Lyn Elizabeth M. Martin, MLS (No. 51/52, 1995). *"A powerful collection authored by respected practitioners who have stormed the bibliographic instruction (BI) trenches and, luckily for us, have recounted their successes and shortcomings." (The Journal of Academic Librarianship)*

Library Users and Reference Services, edited by Jo Bell Whitlatch, PhD (No. 49/50, 1995). *"Well-planned, balanced, and informative. . . . Both new and seasoned professionals will find material for service attitude formation and practical advice for the front lines of service." (Anna M. Donnelly, MS, MA, Associate Professor and Reference Librarian, St. John's University Library)*

Social Science Reference Services, edited by Pam Baxter, MLS (No. 48, 1995). *"Offers practical guidance to the reference librarian. . . . A valuable source of information about specific literatures within the social sciences and the skills and techniques needed to provide access to those literatures." (Nancy P. O'Brien, MLS, Head, Education and Social Science Library, and Professor of Library Administration, University of Illinois at Urbana-Champaign)*

Reference Services in the Humanities, edited by Judy Reynolds, MLS (No. 47, 1994). *"A well-chosen collection of situations and challenges encountered by reference librarians in the humanities." (College Research Library News)*

Racial and Ethnic Diversity in Academic Libraries: Multicultural Issues, edited by Deborah A. Curry, MLS, MA, Susan Griswold Blandy, MEd, and Lyn Elizabeth M. Martin, MLS (No. 45/46, 1994). *"The useful techniques and attractive strategies presented here will provide the incentive for fellow professionals in academic libraries around the country to go and do likewise in their own institutions." (David Cohen, Adjunct Professor of Library Science, School of Library and Information Science, Queens College; Director, EMIE (Ethnic Materials Information Exchange); Editor, EMIE Bulletin)*

School Library Reference Services in the 90s: Where We Are, Where We're Heading, edited by Carol Truett, PhD (No. 44, 1994). *"Unique and valuable to the the teacher-librarian as well as students of librarianship. . . . The overall work successfully interweaves the concept of the continuously changing role of the teacher-librarian." (Emergency Librarian)*

Reference Services Planning in the 90s, edited by Gail Z. Eckwright, MLS, and Lori M. Keenan, MLS (No. 43, 1994). *"This monograph is well-researched and definitive, encompassing reference service as practices by library and information scientists. . . . It should be required reading for all professional librarian trainees." (Feliciter)*

Librarians on the Internet: Impact on Reference Services, edited by Robin Kinder, MLS (No. 41/42, 1994). *"Succeeds in demonstrating that the Internet is becoming increasingly a challenging but practical and manageable tool in the reference librarian's ever-expanding armory." (Reference Reviews)*

Reference Service Expertise, edited by Bill Katz (No. 40, 1993). *This important volume presents a wealth of practical ideas for improving the art of reference librarianship.*

Modern Library Technology and Reference Services, edited by Samuel T. Huang, MLS, MS (No. 39, 1993). *"This book packs a surprising amount of information into a relatively few number of pages. . . . This book will answer many questions." (Science Books and Films)*

Assessment and Accountability in Reference Work, edited by Susan Griswold Blandy, Lyn M. Martin, and Mary L. Strife (No. 38, 1992). *"An important collection of well-written, real-world chapters addressing the central questions that surround performance and services in all libraries." (Library Times International)*

The Reference Librarian and Implications of Mediation, edited by M. Keith Ewing, MLS, and Robert Hauptman, MLS (No. 37, 1992). *"An excellent and thorough analysis of reference mediation. . . . Well worth reading by anyone involved in the delivery of reference services." (Fred Batt, MLS, Associate University Librarian for Public Services, California State University, Sacramento)*

Library Services for Career Planning, Job Searching and Employment Opportunities, edited by Byron Anderson, MA, MLS (No. 36, 1992). *"An interesting book which tells professional libraries how to set up career information centers. . . . Clearly valuable reading for anyone establishing a career library." (Career Opportunities News)*

In the Spirit of 1992: Access to Western European Libraries and Literature, edited by Mary M. Huston, PhD, and Maureen Pastine, MLS (No. 35, 1992). *"A valuable and practical [collection] which every subject specialist in the field would do well to consult." (Western European Specialists Section Newsletter)*

Access Services: The Convergence of Reference and Technical Services, edited by Gillian M. McCombs, ALA (No. 34, 1992). *"Deserves a wide readership among both technical and public services librarians. . . . Highly recommended for any librarian interested in how reference and technical services roles may be combined." (Library Resources & Technical Services)*

Opportunities for Reference Services: The Bright Side of Reference Services in the 1990s, edited by Bill Katz (No. 33, 1991). *"A well-deserved look at the brighter side of reference services. . . . Should be read by reference librarians and their administrators in all types of libraries." (Library Times International)*

Government Documents and Reference Services, edited by Robin Kinder, MLS (No. 32, 1991). *Discusses access possibilities and policies with regard to government information, covering such important topics as new and impending legislation, information on most frequently used and requested sources, and grant writing.*

The Reference Library User: Problems and Solutions, edited by Bill Katz (No. 31, 1991). *"Valuable information and tangible suggestions that will help us as a profession look critically at our users and decide how they are best served." (Information Technology and Libraries)*

Continuing Education of Reference Librarians, edited by Bill Katz (No. 30/31, 1990). *"Has something for everyone interested in this field. . . . Library trainers and library school teachers may well find stimulus in some of the programs outlined here." (Library Association Record)*

Weeding and Maintenance of Reference Collections, edited by Sydney J. Pierce, PhD, MLS (No. 29, 1990). *"This volume may spur you on to planned activity before lack of space dictates 'ad hoc' solutions." (New Library World)*

Serials and Reference Services, edited by Robin Kinder, MLS, and Bill Katz (No. 27/28, 1990). *"The concerns and problems discussed are those of serials and reference librarians everywhere. . . . The writing is of a high standard and the book is useful and entertaining. . . . This book can be recommended." (Library Association Record)*

Rothstein on Reference: . . . with some help from friends, edited by Bill Katz and Charles Bunge, PhD, MLS (No. 25/26, 1990). *"An important and stimulating collection of essays on reference librarianship. . . . Highly recommended!" (Richard W. Grefrath, MA, MLS, Reference Librarian, University of Nevada Library)* Dedicated to the work of Sam Rothstein, one of the world's most respected teachers of reference librarians, this special volume features his writings as well as articles written about him and his teachings by other professionals in the field.

Integrating Library Use Skills Into the General Education Curriculum, edited by Maureen Pastine, MLS, and Bill Katz (No. 24, 1989). *"All contributions are written and presented to a high standard with excellent references at the end of each. . . . One of the best summaries I have seen on this topic." (Australian Library Review)*

Expert Systems in Reference Services, edited by Christine Roysdon, MLS, and Howard D. White, PhD, MLS (No. 23, 1989). *"The single most comprehensive work on the subject of expert systems in reference service." (Information Processing and Management)*

Information Brokers and Reference Services, edited by Bill Katz and Robin Kinder, MLS (No. 22, 1989). *"An excellent tool for reference librarians and indispensable for anyone seriously considering their own information-brokering service." (Booklist)*

Information and Referral in Reference Services, edited by Marcia Stucklen Middleton, MLS, and Bill Katz (No. 21, 1988). *Investigates a wide variety of situations and models which fall under the umbrella of information and referral.*

Reference Services and Public Policy, edited by Richard Irving, MLS, and Bill Katz (No. 20, 1988). *Looks at the relationship between public policy and information and reports ways in which libraries respond to the need for public policy information.*

Finance, Budget, and Management for Reference Services, edited by Ruth A. Fraley, MLS, MBA, and Bill Katz (No. 19, 1989). *"Interesting and relevant to the current state of financial needs in reference service. . . . A must for anyone new to or already working in the reference service area." (Riverina Library Review)*

Current Trends in Information: Research and Theory, edited by Bill Katz and Robin Kinder, MLS (No. 18, 1987). *"Practical direction to improve reference services and does so in a variety of ways ranging from humorous and clever metaphoric comparisons to systematic and practical methodological descriptions." (American Reference Books Annual)*

International Aspects of Reference and Information Services, edited by Bill Katz and Ruth A. Fraley, MLS, MBA (No. 17, 1987). *"An informative collection of essays written by eminent librarians, library school staff, and others concerned with the international aspects of information work." (Library Association Record)*

Reference Services Today: From Interview to Burnout, edited by Bill Katz and Ruth A. Fraley, MLS, MBA (No. 16, 1987). *Authorities present important advice to all reference librarians on the improvement of service and the enhancement of the public image of reference services.*

The Publishing and Review of Reference Sources, edited by Bill Katz and Robin Kinder, MLS (No. 15, 1987). *"A good review of current reference reviewing and publishing trends in the United States . . . will be of interest to intending reviewers, reference librarians, and students." (Australasian College Libraries)*

Personnel Issues in Reference Services, edited by Bill Katz and Ruth Fraley, MLS, MBA (No. 14, 1986). *"Chock-full of information that can be applied to most reference settings. Recommended for libraries with active reference departments." (RQ)*

Reference Services in Archives, edited by Lucille Whalen (No. 13, 1986). *"Valuable for the insights it provides on the reference process in archives and as a source of information on the different ways of carrying out that process." (Library and Information Science Annual)*

Conflicts in Reference Services, edited by Bill Katz and Ruth A. Fraley, MLS, MBA (No. 12, 1985). *This collection examines issues pertinent to the reference department.*

Evaluation of Reference Services, edited by Bill Katz and Ruth A. Fraley, MLS, MBA (No. 11, 1985). *"A much-needed overview of the present state of the art vis-à-vis reference service evaluation. . . . Excellent. . . . Will appeal to reference professionals and aspiring students." (RQ)*

Library Instruction and Reference Services, edited by Bill Katz and Ruth A. Fraley, MLS, MBA (No. 10, 1984). *"Well written, clear, and exciting to read. This is an important work recommended for all librarians, particularly those involved in, interested in, or considering bibliographic instruction. . . . A milestone in library literature." (RQ)*

Reference Services and Technical Services: Interactions in Library Practice, edited by Gordon Stevenson and Sally Stevenson (No. 9, 1984). *"New ideas and longstanding problems are handled with humor and sensitivity as practical suggestions and new perspectives are suggested by the authors." (Information Retrieval & Library Automation)*

Reference Services for Children and Young Adults, edited by Bill Katz and Ruth A. Fraley, MLS, MBA (No. 7/8, 1983). *"Offers a well-balanced approach to reference service for children and young adults." (RQ)*

Video to Online: Reference Services in the New Technology, edited by Bill Katz and Ruth A. Fraley, MLS, MBA (No. 5/6, 1983). *"A good reference manual to have on hand. . . . Well-written, concise, provide[s] a wealth of information." (Online)*

Ethics and Reference Services, edited by Bill Katz and Ruth A. Fraley, MLS, MBA (No. 4, 1982). *Library experts discuss the major ethical and legal implications that reference librarians must take into consideration when handling sensitive inquiries about confidential material.*

Reference Services Administration and Management, edited by Bill Katz and Ruth A. Fraley, MLS, MBA (No. 3, 1982). *Librarianship experts discuss the management of the reference function in libraries and information centers, outlining the responsibilities and qualifications of reference heads.*

Reference Services in the 1980s, edited by Bill Katz (No. 1/2, 1982). *Here is a thought-provoking volume on the future of reference services in libraries, with an emphasis on the challenges and needs that have come about as a result of automation.*

The Image and Role of the Librarian

Wendi Arant, MLS
Candace R. Benefiel, MA, MLIS
Editors

The Image and Role of the Librarian has been co-published simultaneously as *The Reference Librarian*, Number 78 2002.

The Haworth Information Press
An Imprint of
The Haworth Press, Inc.
New York • London • Oxford

Published by

The Haworth Information Press®, 10 Alice Street, Binghamton, NY 13904-1580 USA

The Haworth Information Press® is an imprint of The Haworth Press, Inc., 10 Alice Street, Binghamton, NY 13904-1580 USA.

The Image and Role of the Librarian has been co-published simultaneously as *The Reference Librarian*, Number 78 2002.

The development, preparation, and publication of this work has been undertaken with great care. However, the publisher, employees, editors, and agents of The Haworth Press and all imprints of The Haworth Press, Inc., including The Haworth Medical Press® and Pharmaceutical Products Press®, are not responsible for any errors contained herein or for consequences that may ensue from use of materials or information contained in this work. Opinions expressed by the author(s) are not necessarily those of The Haworth Press, Inc. With regard to case studies, identities and circumstances of individuals discussed herein have been changed to protect confidentiality. Any resemblance to actual persons, living or dead, is entirely coincidental.

Cover design by Brooke R. Stiles.

Library of Congress Cataloging-in-Publication Data

The image and role of the librarian / Wendi Arant, Candace R. Benefiel, editors.
    p. cm.
    Co-published simultaneously as The reference librarian, no. 78, 2002.
    Includes bibliographical references and index.
    ISBN 0-7890-2098-X (alk. paper) – ISBN 0-7890-2099-8 (pbk. : alk. paper)
    1. Librarians–Public opinion. 2. Librarians–Psychology. 3. Library science–Forecasting. I. Arant, Wendi. II. Benefiel, Candace R. III. Reference librarian.
Z682.I43 2003
020′.92–dc21
                                                      2002155850

Indexing, Abstracting & Website/Internet Coverage

This section provides you with a list of major indexing & abstracting services. That is to say, each service began covering this periodical during the year noted in the right column. Most Websites which are listed below have indicated that they will either post, disseminate, compile, archive, cite or alert their own Website users with research-based content from this work. (This list is as current as the copyright date of this publication.)

(continued)

Special bibliographic notes related to special journal issues (separates) and indexing/abstracting:

- indexing/abstracting services in this list will also cover material in any "separate" that is co-published simultaneously with Haworth's special thematic journal issue or DocuSerial. Indexing/abstracting usually covers material at the article/chapter level.
- monographic co-editions are intended for either non-subscribers or libraries which intend to purchase a second copy for their circulating collections.
- monographic co-editions are reported to all jobbers/wholesalers/approval plans. The source journal is listed as the "series" to assist the prevention of duplicate purchasing in the same manner utilized for books-in-series.
- to facilitate user/access services all indexing/abstracting services are encouraged to utilize the co-indexing entry note indicated at the bottom of the first page of each article/chapter/contribution.
- this is intended to assist a library user of any reference tool (whether print, electronic, online, or CD-ROM) to locate the monographic version if the library has purchased this version but not a subscription to the source journal.
- individual articles/chapters in any Haworth publication are also available through the Haworth Document Delivery Service (HDDS).

The Image and Role of the Librarian

CONTENTS

ABOUT THE EDITORS

Wendi Arant is Outreach Services Librarian at Texas A&M University Libraries. She received a BA in Humanities and Romance Languages from the University of Oregon and her Master's of Librarianship from the University of Washington. She has written widely on liaison, outreach and public service issues, appearing in the *Journal of Academic Librarianship*, *Library Administration and Management* and the *Journal of Library Administration*.

Candace R. Benefiel is Senior Humanities Reference Librarian and English Selector at Texas A&M University General Libraries. She has a BA in classics from Rice University, an MLIS from the University of Texas, and an MA in English from West Texas State University. She is currently pursuing a doctoral degree in English at Texas A&M University. Her articles have appeared in *College and Research Libraries*, *Wilson Library Bulletin*, *American Libraries*, *Reference Services Review*, and other library journals. She is also a poet, specializing in mythological themes, and has published poetry in *Classical Outlook*, *Borderlands*, the *Concho River Review*, *Analecta*, and other journals.

Introduction

Wendi Arant
Candace R. Benefiel

It seems that every profession has a natural interest in its universal image and a tendency toward self-examination. For example, the engineering profession is particularly concerned with licensing and qualifications, the medical profession pays special attention to credentials and training, even lawyers are obsessed with issues surrounding their professional identity, right down to being those most likely to tell a lawyer joke.

For all of this professional navel-gazing, there seems to be no profession as preoccupied with self-examination as that of librarianship. While some of it may stem from an identity crisis, the refrain heard over and over is startlingly similar to Dangerfield's "I don't get no respect." This seems to be true of all types of librarians, from public librarians who (often rightly) complain of being treated like servants by the patrons they serve to academic librarians who are always trying to establish their "faculty-ness" to the teaching professors.

In this volume, our article contributors address all aspects of professional identity with regard to librarianship: professional roles, cultural images, popular perceptions and future trends. They examine historical representations, stereotypes and popular culture icons, the roles they play with regard to patron relationships and the outlook for the types of services they may provide in the future.

PROFESSIONAL ROLES

As a so-called service profession, there is often this need to justify the "professional-ness" of librarians. Perhaps this is due to the fact that

[Haworth co-indexing entry note]: "Introduction." Arant, Wendi, and Candace R. Benefiel. Co-published simultaneously in *The Reference Librarian* (The Haworth Information Press, an imprint of The Haworth Press, Inc.) No. 78. 2002. pp. 1-4; and: *The Image and Role of the Librarian* (ed: Wendi Arant, and Candace R. Benefiel) The Haworth Information Press, an imprint of The Haworth Press, Inc., 2002, pp. 1-4. Single or multiple copies of this article are available for a fee from The Haworth Document Delivery Service [1-800-HAWORTH, 9:00 a.m. - 5:00 p.m. (EST). E-mail address: docdelivery@haworthpress.com].

http://www.haworthpress.com/store/product.asp?sku=J120
10.1300/J120v37n78_01

there is no certification such as there is for other professions, like engineers–or maybe, it is because the terminal degree of a master's in library science somehow falls short of the doctorate required of doctors and lawyers. In any case, librarians seem to be forever comparing themselves to these aforementioned occupations and finding themselves lacking (and suspecting that others do too). While lawyers, doctors, engineers and even manicurists are all registered or certified in some way by an impartial entity (thus achieving self-validation), librarians have no licensing procedure, no test to pass–those 3 small initials are all that distinguishes a librarian from a library classified staff person or even a library student worker, especially in the eyes of the public. And, of course, in the case of school librarians, there is not necessarily the requirement of an MLS. Certainly expertise does enter into the picture, but without standards of practice (which for other professions are generally set by the governing boards), there is very little consistency from place to place, or even within the same library or department.

The services and functions that librarians provide in their day-to-day work and the value they play to those they serve are often overlooked, by both those inside and outside the profession. In an effort to provide what is now referred to as transparent service, they have rendered themselves, and in turn their service contributions, largely invisible to their clientele.

- Gary Mason Church examines this phenomenon as well as other widely-held public and academic opinions of librarians in "In the Eye of the Beholder: How Librarians Have Been Viewed Over Time."
- Daniel Liestman takes a new twist on this approach, looking at the historical view and what 19th century scholars speculated the future of the profession would hold, with "Looking Back to the Future: Turn of the Last Century Librarians Look Ahead to the Twentieth Century."

CULTURAL IMAGES

Where Marion the Librarian was once the generally accepted stereotype (exemplified by librarians in films such as Shirley Jones in *The Music Man* and Donna Reed, saved from a life of librarian-spinsterhood by Jimmy Stewart, in *It's a Wonderful Life*), Giles the Librarian (of "Buffy the Vampire Slayer" fame) has gained enough popularity that he appeared on a cover of *American Libraries*. The occasional cranky, old (and unsympathetic) spinster librarian (recently resurrected in the form of Jocasta Nu, the Jedi Librarian in *Star Wars Episode II: Attack of the Clones*) still appears. Perhaps the ultimate "live reference chat" librarian surfaced in the form of New York Public Library's Vox, in 2002's *The Time Machine*, a holographic interface who instantly produced books on any topic, sang Broadway show tunes in multipart harmony, and never (EVER) forgot a patron.

- Jeanine Williamson's "Jungian/Myers-Briggs Personality Types of Librarians in Films" presents an array of the cinematic portrayal of the profession, from the stereotypic to more original characters, discussing the most prevalent characteristics.
- Following that vein of popular culture iconography, Doug Highsmith looks at librarians and the role they play in various comic books. "The Long, Strange Trip of Barbara Gordon: Images of Librarians in Comic Books" looks at a number of classic as well as some of the more fringe comic book characters.
- With a slightly more traditional perspective, Elaine Yontz does a parallel study of "Librarians in Children's Literature, 1909-2000."

POPULAR PERCEPTIONS

The image of the librarian seems to have come full-circle, historically speaking. Initially, the profession was peopled by introverted, bookish men, although certain exceptions stood out–Casanova, for an example against stereotype, for one, and Hypatia, a philosopher and librarian in 5th century Alexandria, for another. Librarianship, especially at the end of the 19th century under the guidance of Melvil Dewey, slowly transformed into a "woman's profession," a label it has retained even to the present. With the growth of the Internet, the image has come around again to the bookish men (or women) as if the evolution of information into the electronic format has evolved librarians into a type of computer geek.

- Thad E. Dickinson takes a look at the men in the profession (who incidentally are heavily in the minority) with his "Looking at the Male Librarian Stereotype."
- Beth Posner's "Know-It-All Librarians" looks at the myth behind the perceived omniscience of librarians.

- Jody Fagan examines "Students' Perceptions of Academic Librarians."

FUTURE TRENDS

Now, more than any other time in history, librarianship is in a state of transition. The Internet has had a profound impact on the resources and services that librarians of all kinds provide to their patrons. Electronic information has transformed the roles and responsibilities of librarians, even to the point of revolutionizing library education and service expectations.

- Johnnieque B. Love surveys specialist librarians in "The Enhanced and Changing Role of the Specialist Librarian: Survey of Education Librarians."
- And finally, as if a logical next step to Liestman's examination of the future of librarianship from the view of the 19th century, Pixey Anne Mosley speculates on the role that Generation X will play in the future of the profession.

While such introspective examination of professional roles and responsibilities, patron expectations and perceptions, popular stereotypes and historical/cultural images might be considered self-serving, it is to be hoped that a presentation of these views of librarianship might bring some clarity and recognition, in addition to sparking some debate and raising other questions to ponder.

PROFESSIONAL ROLES

In the Eye of the Beholder: How Librarians Have Been Viewed Over Time

Gary Mason Church

SUMMARY. As with beauty and other concepts, librarians have been viewed in many subjective ways. On the other hand, some attempts have also been made to obtain more objective views of librarians. This paper provides a summary of these views, or images, that extend back to the early 18th century. It presents the many traits that comprise these images, the sources or origins of the images, the various groups that hold the images, and ends with a reason why current images are indefinite and "blurry." *[Article copies available for a fee from The Haworth Document Delivery Service: 1-800-HAWORTH. E-mail address: <docdelivery@haworthpress. com> Website: <http://www.HaworthPress.com> © 2002 by The Haworth Press, Inc. All rights reserved.]*

Gary Mason Church is affiliated with Montgomery College Library, 3200 College Park Drive, Building F, Room 165, Conroe, TX 77584 (E-mail: gary.m.church@ nhmccd.edu).

[Haworth co-indexing entry note]: "In the Eye of the Beholder: How Librarians Have Been Viewed Over Time." Church, Gary Mason. Co-published simultaneously in *The Reference Librarian* (The Haworth Information Press, an imprint of The Haworth Press, Inc.) No. 78, 2002, pp. 5-24; and: *The Image and Role of the Librarian* (ed: Wendi Arant, and Candace R. Benefiel) The Haworth Information Press, an imprint of The Haworth Press, Inc., 2002, pp. 5-24. Single or multiple copies of this article are available for a fee from The Haworth Document Delivery Service [1-800-HAWORTH, 9:00 a.m. - 5:00 p.m. (EST). E-mail address: docdelivery@haworthpress.com].

KEYWORDS. Academic librarians, faculty, faculty perceptions of librarians, faculty rank, faculty status, faculty surveys, librarian characteristics, librarian-faculty relationships, librarian image, librarian roles, librarian self-image, librarianship, library buildings, library profession, media portrayals of librarians, personality tests, public librarians, public perceptions of librarians, questionnaires

Unlearned men, of books assume the care, As eunuchs are the guardian of the fair.

–Edward Young, 1728

INTRODUCTION

Young's quote portrays librarians as uneducated, male caretakers of books. Fortunately, his image or mental picture of librarians is only one of many that have existed over the years. The literature shows that these images ascribe a variety of traits to librarians, and many of them portray librarians in a more favorable manner than Young. As we will see, there is a thin line between the image of *the librarian* and that of *the person* who happens to be a librarian. Many of the images revealed derive from second-hand knowledge, abstract ideas of what a librarian should be, and not concrete, first-hand experience with librarians.

The images described here have been held by the general public, higher-education faculty, and librarians themselves, as well as presented in the media. They primarily address academic librarians with some attention to special and public librarians. The images relate to librarian responsibilities, roles, traits (e.g., gender), and faculty relationships, as well as the issue of faculty rank and what librarianship offers as a profession. The impressions originate from sources including direct interaction with librarians, hearsay, and media portrayals of librarians. They are further defined and refined with techniques such as personality tests and faculty surveys. In this manner, we strive to refine the image, to remove from this image the inaccuracies of hearsay, misinterpretation, and misperception, to objectify the subjective.

PUBLIC IMAGES OF THE LIBRARIAN

The general public has some stereotyped images of the librarian. One is presented by Johnson (1990), a newspaper columnist. In his article about the 1990 American Library Association (ALA) Annual Conference, he commented that instead of the inaccurate image of librarians as either "meek, underpaid, overly fussy old ladies" or "cops who happen to understand the Dewey Decimal System," a librarian is more accurately "an outspoken, extraordinarily well-educated civil libertarian who also is a technological whiz and might very well be male." At the time of this conference, Patricia Berger was ALA president. In this same article, President Berger mentioned the reason a local hotel official liked doing business with librarians. The official said, "You honor your reservations; you go to your meetings so we can clean the rooms; you're relatively quiet; and you drink more than the American Legion" (Johnson 1990, 1).

Leigh and Sewny (1960) present another public image, ranging from

> the very favorable picture of the scholarly, "resourceful" professional who is accessible, friendly, skilled, and eager to help the library user, and who discovers for him the materials he needs but knows not of, to the picture of the "timid, plain-looking female, conservative morally and politically, middle-aged or older . . . busily stamping *her* [italics added] 3 × 5 cards and collecting pennies for overdue books." (Leigh and Sewny 1960, 2090)

Leigh and Sewny (1960) also relate an image of the librarian as described by an English professor at Harvard University. The professor commented that

> To single ladies librarianship offers status, some security, and a sense of civic virtues. This is not to say that all librarians are maiden ladies, but enough of them are to rank librarians with school teachers, YWCA secretaries, and social workers as persons less likely to go to nightclubs than are receptionists or department-store buyers. . . . A librarian too often resembles a head-waiter showing one to a table in a large restaurant and too little resembles an artist having profound and passionate views of life, death and immortality. (Leigh and Sewny 1960, 2091)

They go on to say that these images of the librarian

> are the products of the varying perceptions of regular users of good libraries, of occasional users of poor libraries, of those whose library contacts were limited to childhood experiences in small

communities, and of persons whose image depends on hearsay and the stock caricatures of the mass media. (Leigh and Sewny 1960, 2090)

Place the librarian and the interaction in an environment other than a library, or even in different libraries, and the image would be different. However, would that image then be of the librarian or the person who is the librarian?

LIBRARIAN SELF-IMAGES

The literature also contains self-images of the librarian, or those images provided by librarians. In her discussion of the work of Robert Douglass, Holbrook (1968) mentions his investigation of librarians' self-image. From a review of pertinent articles, he concluded that

> on the whole, the librarians were more openly and severely critical of themselves and of their colleagues than were their laymen critics. It may be suspected that self-depreciation is found among librarians to a greater extent than among other professional groups. The self-condemnatory nature of many of the articles was so pronounced, in fact, as to produce a tonal effect of almost masochistic quality. (in Holbrook 1968, 181)

In her discussion of Rupert Giles, DeCandido (1999) provides–though not presented as such–two examples of librarian self-images, her own and that of Lesley Knieriem, a reference librarian at a public library. DeCandido (1999, 46) reveals her self-image when she states that

> we came to librarianship because we loved the sound of words talking to each other, rubbing up against each other; or because the world inside a story was far more real to us than the world inside our neighborhoods; or because we loved chasing an idea around. For many of us, librarianship originally was a choice to separate ourselves from workplaces that were less humane, less involved in the drama of people's lives.

Knieriem's self-image of the librarian is revealed when she comments that

Giles is appealing to librarians in that he portrays us as we like to think we are: enormously intelligent, literate, genteel, sensitive, devoted to our patrons, with a sexy, ferocious "ripper" concealed within, only to be let out when needed to slay the demons of ignorance. Yes, he does fit many of the stereotypes: bookish, stuffy, reserved, technophobic (this last isn't any of us!). (DeCandido 1999, 47)

IMAGES DERIVED FROM SETTING

Compared to Edward Young's portrayal of the librarian, Hart, Bains, and Jones (1996) present a much more flattering–even exalted–image. In their fascinating article, they discuss how the design of public library *buildings* not only creates a cultural image of knowledge, but also an image of the librarian within those buildings. Round library buildings, for example, have a panopticon (all-seeing) nature that also defines and colors the image of the librarian.

Seated at the center, the place and status is ascribed to the librarian. The place is at the center of knowledge; the status is that of a guardian and gatekeeper to knowledge. The imposing structure of the building in the round is conveyed on to the librarian. . . . Having control of access to the tools of knowledge . . . the librarian is more than a custodian of the place and its contents. The librarian has the power to regulate, monitor and control the use of books and the users of the library. Stated simply the librarian is able to exercise total surveillance. . . . they can see all and, by their visible presence and central place, communicate to all that enter, that they are subject to the custodian's gaze. (Hart, Banes, and Jones 1996, 28)

Technologies in addition to library building design also impact the image of librarians. Because of the Internet as a portal to pornography, "the role of librarian now includes thwarting sex acts on the premises" of public libraries (Downey 2000, 50).

IMAGES OF THE ACADEMIC LIBRARIAN

Much has been written about higher-education faculty members' image of and relationship with academic librarians. Marchant (1969) briefly discusses the history of librarianship and the conflict between faculty and librarians. Biggs (1981) also comments briefly on historical aspects of librarianship. She states that "conscientious academic library administrators [who] began to emerge slowly in the nineteenth century [mostly] remained 'bookmen' at heart and [were] more interested in enriching the library than in systematising it and facilitating its use" (Biggs 1981, 183-184). She also relates an 1876 comment by Lloyd P. Smith of the Philadelphia Library Company who believed that

> the first requisite for success in our vocation is . . . a natural love for books. A librarian should be . . . consumed by an insatiable thirst for knowledge, and interested in a wide range of subjects. A knowledge of the outsides of books is not sufficient . . . a librarian's evenings should, by choice, be spent in reading. (Biggs 1981, 184)

Danton (1936) emphasizes how faculty and librarians interact as they perform the important task of selecting books for the collection. He comments that college librarians devote a lot of time and thought to selecting books and that they are well qualified for and genuinely interested in this task. Furthermore, Danton goes on to say that faculty members appreciate the librarian's efforts to build the collection in their respective disciplines.

Barzun (1946) compares the role of the academic librarian to that of someone who systematically distributes desirable goods to an anonymous public who knows little about the system. He stresses that the two most important traits of the librarian are general knowledge and attentiveness to patron needs. Librarians should also be tactful, patient, intuitive, mentally quick, calm, collected, sympathetic, and scholarly. Barzun (1946, 117) also objects to the phrase "library service" because it

> reminds me unpleasantly of service stations for gasoline and oil. These are books that we are dealing with, and I want, not library service, but librarianship–a fit parallel to musicianship. You do not say, "The Budapest Quartette gives excellent musical service."

Holley (1961) discusses effective relationships between librarians and faculty members. He says the service librarians give faculty should be "activist, participation-conscious, direct-aid-giving . . . with even an occasional bit of pampering thrown in" (Holley 1961, 732). He also believes the librarian's first responsibility is to work with the faculty.

Tannenbaum (1963, 248) reviews how librarians are portrayed in academic novels as a way to discover the librarian's "true image in the halls of learning." He believes that librarians are very concerned about the image they have in their particular community. Regarding their appearance in academic novels, Tannenbaum (1963, 249) comments that

> librarians themselves are rarely mentioned; if they are it is usually within the pejorative framework of a current cliché. No librarian has a role of even minor importance . . . In most of these novels he does not exist except as an anonymous wraith.

He interprets this to mean that

> librarians are not important in the academic worlds portrayed in these novels; they are scarcely noticed. . . . [They] do not make good dramatic material. . . . So it can be argued that the librarian is a colorless, efficient person whose books and duties seem to provide perfect camouflage for *him* [italics added].

However, is Tannenbaum correct? Do novels–*fictional* prose narratives–reveal *true* images?

In her attempt to gather information about the image of the academic librarian, Holbrook (1968) searched educational and library journals and sociological examinations of various professions. She also surveyed members of the English faculty at the University of Kentucky. The image she discovered includes the following characteristics:

- The librarian's "mental activity is continuous, impassioned, versatile, and altogether insignificant. He abounds in useless analogies and fruitless scruples" (Holbrook 1968, 174).
- Robert Douglass investigated the librarian personality and claims the stereotype of the librarian includes the categories of "1. Orderliness, meticulousness, acquisitiveness. 2. Conformity, conservatism. 3. Passivity, submissiveness. 4. Introspection, non-social attitudes and behavior. 5. Anxiousness; lack of self-confidence" (Holbrook 1968, 175).

Holbrook (1968) also mentions that, in his 1947-48 study, Douglass used a questionnaire and five personality tests to gather data on the distinctive qualities of librarians. The personality tests at least partially supported the following hypotheses (Holbrook 1968, 180):

- *Hypothesis 1*. The librarian is more orderly, meticulous, neat and compulsive in behavior than people in general.
- *Hypothesis 2*. The librarian is more conscientious, scrupulous, and conforming, and less innovative and creative than people in general.
- *Hypothesis 3*. The librarian is more deferential, submissive, and respectful of authority than people in general.
- *Hypothesis 4*. The librarian is more self-contained, self-sufficient, preoccupied with subjective feelings, introspective, introverted, and non-social than people in general.
- *Hypothesis 7*. The male librarian is more feminine in his interest than men in general.

The tests did not generally support these two hypotheses:

- *Hypothesis 5*. The librarian is more anxious and less self-confident than people in general.
- *Hypothesis 6*. The librarian is more neurotic than people in general.

In her discussion of the conflict between academic librarians and faculty members, Biggs (1981) also mentions the work of Douglass. She states that

> he remarked in passing that "many of the traits which characterize the modal librarian . . . are not those most closely associated with or productive of forceful leadership, distinguished scholarship, imaginative research, or other highly creative attainments." Douglass hypothesized that the stereotype was drawn "very largely from popular images of the middle-aged woman librarian," and writers from both librarianship and the teaching profession have focused on the female majority in librarianship as a particular problem when librarians seek to be taken seriously and accepted as peers. (Biggs 1981, 192)

Holbrook (1968) also comments on faculty rank or status for academic librarians. She states that "while faculty members in theory accept librarians as their academic equals, in the actual practice their judgment of librarians' scholarliness contains implicit qualifying statements that suggest a very probable falling short of the scholarly mark" (Holbrook 1968, 187). She goes on to relate a warning by Robert

Vosper who remarked, "I have a frank feeling that too many librarians want something called academic status without really being willing to face up to the responsibilities involved" (Holbrook 1968, 187-188). Along these same lines, Blackburn (1968, 173) comments that "faculty rank seems to be a sought after goal almost as an end in itself. . . . A faculty member cannot like an administrator, and that is what a librarian is."

Blackburn (1968) also identifies sources of conflict between faculty and academic libraries/librarians. He believes this conflict partly arises from differences in the personalities and roles of faculty and librarians. According to Blackburn (1968, 173), the traits of

> order, efficiency, and economy and the like seem to be predominant in librarians. . . . Then there is the predominant maleness of faculty versus the predominant femaleness of librarians and the associations these bring forth (as in, say, doctor versus nurse). Punctuality, rules and regulations . . . are integrated in a librarian's life.

Regarding roles, Blackburn (1968, 174) states that "librarians are in a servant role."

In Marchant's (1969) discussion of the conflict between faculty and librarian, he also broaches the topic of faculty rank for academic librarians. He mentions that

> librarians want to be considered as faculty and thus legitimatize their role as part of the instructional process. . . . The faculty, however, equates the librarian with the administrator, the natural enemy of professors, and resists this aspiration. In addition, senior faculty feel that giving faculty status to librarians would water down its image because of the lower educational norm of librarians. . . . The library's primary purpose, in their eyes, is to serve the faculty. . . . They are humiliated to have to ask for help from the lower-status librarian. (Marchant 1969, 2887)

As further insight into the faculty's perception of the academic librarian, Marchant (1969, 2888) comments that "the faculty projects upon the librarian the false stereotype of 'keeper of the books' to which they wish *her* [italics added] to adhere."

Logsdon (1970) also juxtaposes librarians and scholars and refers to them as eternal enemies. He remarks that librarians are more altruistic than any other profession. To the scholar, the perfect library is one whose top priority is to satisfy his academic needs. According to a law professor at Columbia, the appropriate acquisitions policy for a research library should be to "have the titles I need, when I need them, and of course where I need them. Be sure they go to the law library" (Logsdon 1970, 2872).

Regarding cataloging of library materials, Logsdon (1970, 2873) refers to another professor at Columbia who asked, "Why the backlogs of uncataloged material? Fifteen thousand volumes at Columbia alone. Any graduate student knowing Russian could catalog a hundred titles a day." The professor was simply not aware of all the work that cataloging involves.

Lastly, Logsdon (1970, 2874) relates two viewpoints of librarianship. The first is in a 1929 letter from his older brother who comments on what it would be like for a 17-year-old freshman–Logsdon–to work at the Western Reserve University library.

> The pay at first is paltry and you will not get in more than $5 time each week after classes begin, but nevertheless the future in library work is what counts. Girls graduating from library school start in at $1800 per year and get a month's vacation with pay. Men get more than that, so it may be an opportunity for you if you should like the work. It is nothing for men librarians to make $5000 per year.

The second viewpoint comes from a high-school and junior-college career book from around 1960.

> As you reflect on librarianship as a possible career, you will see a many-faceted and anything but a static, rocking-chair kind of profession. Keep always in mind that because the library is a social institution and as such reflects the society and culture it serves, librarianship must be keenly sensitive to and knowledgeable about the world in which it exists. It is a good life.

The status of the relationship between faculty and librarians at 275 liberal arts colleges was studied by Scherer (1970). He reports that

> most faculty members, administrators, and librarians in this study agreed that it is in the best interests of the college to grant faculty status to professional members of the library staff. . . . In addition, four out of five librarians were given important committee assignments; but, paradoxically, very seldom was the counseling of students, the sponsorship of social groups, or advisement of scholarly organizations entrusted to librarians. (Scherer 1970, 40)

He concludes that "this study discovered almost complete harmony and good will between faculty members and librarians in liberal arts colleges" (Scherer 1970, 43). This contrasts sharply with Logsdon (1970) who refers to faculty member and librarian as eternal enemies.

Davis and Bentley (1979) studied factors that influence the perceptions faculty members have of academic librarians. They discovered that significant differences related to the length of time faculty members had been at an institution. For example, 86 percent of the faculty who had been at an institution for seven or more years rated "the helpfulness of the library staff high in terms of importance to their use of the library" (Davis and Bentley 1979, 530). In comparison, this same rating was given by only 63.6 percent of faculty members who had been at an institution for less than seven years.

Biggs (1981) examined sources of conflict and tension between faculty members and librarians. The increasing size and complexity of academic libraries in the early 1900s created a need for library personnel trained in librarianship. A common solution to this need was to appoint an esteemed faculty member as library director and a librarian as his assistant. At the University of Chicago, when the director stepped down, the faculty did not permit the librarian assistant to take his place. The appointment of those outside the library profession to high positions in research libraries was still a practice until at least the 1940s. Commenting on this practice, Biggs (1981, 185) states that

> this pattern of scholar-librarian and librarian-assistant is fast disappearing, but while it survived it instilled in librarians a bitter contempt and sense of injury. Undoubtedly, the pattern often resulted in a detached, prestigious, and well-paid library director whose underpaid and unappreciated assistant did most of the day-to-day work; undoubtedly, it reflected an assumption about the relative quality of their different backgrounds. . . . Present-day advocacy of "subject specialists" and "second master's degrees" implicitly recognizes the problem of a library staff without knowledge of, and respect for, books and methods of scholarly investigation.

Biggs (1981, 191) also provides some quotations by faculty members, librarians, and others about librarians. These include the following:

- The time has at last come when a librarian may, without assumption, speak of *his* [italics added] occupation as a profession (M. Dewey, librarian, 1876).
- I am doubtful that the librarians will become full-fledged professionals (W. J. Goode, 1961).
- Fundamentally, the librarian may have only one deeply ingrained desire: that is to be recognized as an intellectual. This is *his* [italics added] basic striving, and all of his efforts at status attainment are directed toward it (H. Lancour, library educator, 1961).
- The academic librarian is the ultimate in scholarship and the only unfettered clear voice of the aspiration of the academic community (E. J. Josey, librarian, 1971).
- The librarian seems to have an inordinate passion for status (R. T. Blackburn, higher education professor, 1968).

In addition, Biggs (1981) makes a few statements about how library education is perceived.

> Those both inside and outside the profession have deplored the low research activity and scant analytical thinking among librarians, usually presumed a consequence of the fact that few receive relevant training or encouragement in the course of their professional education. . . . Library school faculty members have been accused of unusually low productivity, and although historical and practical factors enter into this, to the extent that it is true, it creates a barrier to recognition of the equality of library education, and of professionally trained librarians, by other faculty members on campus. (Biggs 1981, 193)

Biggs (1981) also reports on the issue of faculty status for academic librarians. Because library directors commonly came from the faculty in the 19th and early 20th centuries, the status of the head librarian was rarely questioned. However, that of ordinary librarians was seldom, if ever, considered. Faculties frequently resist faculty status for librarians,

> especially on campuses where requirements for appointment, promotion, and tenure are high. . . . However, some librarians call for faculty status *without* faculty rank, and the term "academic status" is also used frequently, occasionally as a synonym for faculty status, but more often to designate a purgatorial state somewhere between the heaven of professorship and the hell of librarianship. . . .

Lacking a clear-cut notion of what "librarian status" might be–indeed, fearing that the phrase may be a contradiction in terms–librarians reach out for the ready-made status of an obviously respected profession. (Biggs 1981, 194-196)

Biggs (1981, 186) summarizes the relationship between librarians and faculty members by saying that

librarians and faculty members were once creatures of the same order, with similar educational preparation, interests, and understanding of what the library should do. Rather quickly they have evolved into quite different creatures, each insistent upon professional autonomy, stubbornly holding sometimes disparate visions of the library's mission, and communicating very little with each other.

Cook (1981) studied how the teaching faculty at Southern Illinois University at Carbondale (SIU-C) perceived the status and contributions of academic librarians. She briefly reviews similar studies and mentions one by Knapp done in the late 1950s that indicated faculty members thought library directors but not ordinary library staff qualified for faculty rank and status. Also, faculty status for librarians increased from 50 to 75 percent from 1966 to 1975.

Cook (1981) also asked faculty members if they thought the academic librarian's primary role should be teaching, research, or service. "Eighty-five percent indicated they perceived the major duties of librarians to be those of service to students and faculty. Eight percent indicated research . . . and 5 percent indicated teaching" (Cook 1981, 219).

When faculty members were asked how they viewed academic librarians, "twenty-eight percent . . . viewed librarians as equal to teaching faculty, whereas 65 percent viewed librarians as professionals, rather than faculty. Only 7 percent . . . viewed librarians as nonprofessional or equal to clerical or secretarial help" (Cook 1981, 219). Of course, these views depend on how well faculty members understand and are aware of what librarians actually do.

When the faculty was asked if academic librarians should have faculty rank and status, 57 percent answered affirmatively, and 43 percent answered negatively.

Of the 148 faculty members indicating that librarians should not have faculty rank and status, 58 percent indicated it was due to insufficient teaching; 40 percent indicated it was due to insufficient research and publications; 13 percent indicated it was due to insufficient service; and 27 percent indicated it was due to insufficient education. The numbers total more than 100 percent because respondents could check multiple reasons for denying librarians faculty rank and status. (Cook 1981, 220)

Cook (1981, 214) believes that "the image and prestige of academic librarians will be based upon their academic preparation, service, and contributions to their colleges and universities."

Faculty perceptions of academic librarians were also studied by Oberg, Schleiter, and Houten (1989). Their survey of the full-time faculty at Albion College included questions from previous surveys in addition to questions of particular interest to college librarians. As in prior similar studies, results varied according to such faculty traits as rank (professors, associate professors, assistant professors, instructors), faculty orientation (teaching, publication), frequency of library use, and academic unit (natural sciences, humanities, social sciences, fine arts). Results of the survey include the following:

- Faculty often fail to distinguish between librarians and support staff (Oberg, Schleiter, and Houten 1989, 217).
- The current study demonstrates that more than two-thirds of our respondents do not consider librarians to be their peers. . . . The faculty cohort most likely to accept librarians as academic equals was from fine arts (50%), followed by the humanities (32%) and, lastly, the social sciences (25%) and the sciences (23%). . . . Of the frequent library users, 32% view librarians as academic equals and 66% as professionals. The equivalent figures for infrequent library users are 23% and 73% respectively (Oberg, Schleiter, and Houten 1989, 223-224).
- To the question, Should librarians be eligible for tenure? and the equivalent question concerning rank and faculty status, an identical 64% responded yes and 36% no (Oberg, Schleiter, and Houten 1989, 224).

Ivey (1994) also studied teaching faculty perceptions of academic librarians, but at Memphis State University (MSU). He lists some factors that constantly influence the faculty-librarian relationship, including "the number of academic librarians, the strength or weakness of the collection, and the size of the institution, the faculty, the student body, and the library facility" (Ivey 1994, 69). He also provides some impressions that faculty members have had of librarians as reported in previous literature. Among these are the following:

- Teaching faculty think they are more qualified to control book selection because of higher intellectual achievement reflected in their doctoral degrees.
- Faculty-librarian relations are frustrating, distant, and ineffective.
- Few faculty think librarians are their equals academically.
- Most faculty members think librarians are professionals, not academics.
- Teaching faculty do not think librarians are essential to an institution's teaching and research mission.

The purpose of Ivey's (1994) study was to identify the incorrect perceptions that faculty have of librarians so those perceptions can be corrected. To gather data about these perceptions, he surveyed almost 400 teaching faculty members at MSU. The survey contained 23 questions either taken from previous studies or created for this one in particular. Results of the survey include the following:

- Only 47 percent of the Memphis State teaching faculty respondents found librarians useful or very useful in keeping them informed of changes in the library. Only 24 percent found librarians useful or very useful in keeping them informed of new publications in their discipline, and only 50 percent found librarians useful or very useful in assisting them in their teaching activities (Ivey, 1994, 72).
- As for librarians' contributions to the education of their students, respondents at Memphis State (62 percent) believe that librarians have some to very substantial involvement in the education of their students. . . . [Thirty-eight] percent believe that librarians have only some involvement in the education of their students. . . . A disappointingly low 23 percent of Memphis State respondents believe that librarians have made more than some contribution to the education of their students. This reflects either low expectations of librarians by teaching faculty or a *misunderstanding of their abilities and responsibilities* [italics added] (Ivey 1994, 73-74).
- Memphis State respondents, when asked to rate librarians' roles on a scale of 1 to 4, highest to lowest priority, give highest priority to university service (57 percent), followed by research (40 percent), public service (19 percent), teaching (16 percent), management (15 percent), and administration (8 percent) (Ivey 1994, 77).

- When asked whether librarians should conduct research, 71 percent of the respondents believe that librarians should conduct some kind of research (Ivey 1994, 77).
- When faculty were asked about the importance of librarians' assistance in faculty research, 70 percent of the respondents replied that librarians were important or very important to their research. Only 14 percent claim that librarians are of little importance or unimportant, while 10 percent are neutral (Ivey 1994, 78).
- Faculty respondents also believe that librarians should have primary or equal responsibility for the selection of general interest books (95 percent). Of the respondents, 65 percent said that librarians and teaching faculty should have primary and shared responsibility for book selection on interdisciplinary subjects. Teaching faculty respondents (76 percent) state that they should control book selection on course-related subjects. Only 9 percent want to share this responsibility with librarians (Ivey 1994, 78).
- This survey reveals that 90 percent of the Memphis State respondents do not believe librarians to be their academic equals. . . . However, 75 percent consider librarians professionals or semi-professionals (paraprofessionals) (Ivey 1994, 79).

Like previous researchers, Ivey (1994) also found that perceptions such as these depended upon various faculty characteristics. These characteristics were faculty rank (e.g., professors, associate professors), faculty orientation (e.g., teaching, research), and frequency of library use (e.g., daily, weekly). For example,

> teaching-oriented respondents at Memphis State rate teaching as a higher priority for librarians (51 percent) than research-oriented (44 percent) or teaching-research oriented respondents (44 percent). A significantly higher portion of teaching-research-oriented faculty see public service as a higher priority for librarians than teaching-oriented faculty. Frequent library users (53 percent) are more likely to assign teaching a high or higher priority than infrequent library users (38 percent). (Ivey 1994, 77)

CONCLUSIONS

The image of the librarian–as described in the literature–has apparently changed over the years and strongly depends on who defines it. In some of the older literature, its components were subjective opinions or general descriptions of the traits librarians either *do* have (e.g., accessible, friendly, skilled, altruistic, less likely to go to nightclubs) or *should* have (e.g., tactful, patient, consumed by an insatiable thirst for knowledge). The image has also been defined by stereotypes of the librarian (e.g., the scholarly, resourceful professional; the timid, plain-looking, middle-aged female; the passive gatekeeper). Some writers have described librarians in favorable terms (e.g., indispensable helper), while others have not (e.g., "intellectual eunuchs" who care for books). Librarians have also been compared to other workers (e.g., school teachers, YWCA secretaries). Still others have investigated the librarian personality to discover traits to add to the image (e.g., orderly, scrupulous, no more neurotic than most folks).

Particular effort has been made to clarify faculty perceptions of the academic librarian. Emphasis has been placed on two issues: relationships with faculty and faculty rank/status. The relationship between academic librarians and teaching faculty has been variously described as appreciative, one of eternal enemies, one of harmony and good will, and one of disparate visions and inadequate communications. Faculty do not universally agree that academic librarians are their equals academically or that they should have faculty rank/status, but significant gains have apparently been made by librarians in this area. Many faculty members think librarians–though not their equals–are professionals whose primary function should be to serve faculty and students. Researchers commonly obtain information about these and other issues with more objective faculty surveys that contain questions designed to clarify faculty perceptions of librarians so steps can be taken to correct misconceptions and improve relationships.

Various authors provide opinions about how to clarify faculty perceptions of the academic librarian. Lanning (1988, 8-9) suggests the following ways to improve the relationship between faculty member and librarian:

- Efforts should be directed to increase the dialogue between librarian and faculty member. At least one faculty member [should be] in each department who recognizes the importance of information literacy skills.
- Librarian and faculty member should work towards a common goal of curriculum development.
- Library personnel must be willing to serve on curriculum development committees and be vocal advocates for their points of view.

- The library and [academic] departments should seek novel approaches to common problems of limited resources and heavy work loads as they affect curriculum development.
- Librarians and faculty should seek opportunities to team teach courses on information literacy.

Oberg, Schleiter, and Houten (1989, 225) state that

> faculty harbor serious *misperceptions about the role and function of librarians* [italics added], underutilize and undervalue their teaching and research skills, and distrust their ability to select books. . . . To change [these misconceptions], librarians will need to communicate a clearer image of who they are and what it is they do.

This statement relates to the comment by Ivey (1994) that teaching faculty may misunderstand the abilities and responsibilities of librarians. Similarly, Divay, Ducas, and Michaud-Oystryk (1987) comment that librarians cannot expect faculty members to fully appreciate their institutional role as long as faculty are unable to clearly distinguish the professionally trained librarian from the rest of the library staff. This relates to the comment by Oberg, Schleiter, and Houten (1989, 217) that "faculty often fail to distinguish between librarians and support staff." Oberg, Schleiter, and Houten (1989, 226) conclude that

> the task before librarians today is to make the invisible visible. They must settle upon their role, perform it consistently, and communicate it unambiguously. When they do, their unique services and abilities will come to be understood and valued by their communities. Librarians may then find their eternal quest for a status appropriate to their contribution that much closer to realization.

This advice seems reasonable. However, the ubiquitous technological change that is sweeping the country impacts library structure and function and puts libraries in a period of transition. For example, electronic access and delivery of information can impact traditional acquisitions and collection development functions (e.g., providing access to materials instead of buying them) and alter the boundaries and relationships between these and other library departments. The transition period is characterized by confusion, fear, and uncertainty about the exact role of libraries and librarians in the future. Although it also presents new opportunities, this period of transition makes it difficult for librarians to "communicate a clearer image of who they are and what it is they do" or "settle upon their role, perform it consistently, and communicate it unambiguously." Today, transition and uncertainty distort the librarian's image so it is unclear to them as well as others.

REFERENCES

Barzun, J. 1946. The scholar looks at the library. *College and Research Libraries* 7:113-117.

Biggs, M. 1981. Sources of tension and conflict between librarians and faculty. *The Journal of Higher Education* 52:182-201.

Blackburn, R. T. 1968. College libraries–indicted failures: Some reasons–and a possible remedy. *College & Research Libraries* 29:171-177.

Cook, M. K. 1981. Rank, status, and contribution of academic librarians as perceived by the teaching faculty at Southern Illinois University, Carbondale. *College & Research Libraries* 42:214-223.

Danton, J. P. 1936. The faculty, the librarian, and book selection. *The Library Journal* 61:715-717.

Davis, J. Y., and S. Bentley. 1979. Factors affecting faculty perceptions of academic libraries. *College & Research Libraries* 40:527-532.

DeCandido, G. A. 1999. Bibliographic good vs. evil in *Buffy the Vampire Slayer. American Libraries* 29 (September):44-47.

Divay, G., A. M. Ducas, and M. Michaud-Oystryck. 1987. Faculty perceptions of librarians at the University of Manitoba. *College & Research Libraries* 48:27-35.

Downey, S. 2000. Not on the reading list. *Newsweek*, 17 July, 50.

Hart, C., M. Bains, and K. Jones. 1996. The myth of material knowledge: Reading the image of library buildings. *New Library World* 97(1127):23-31.

Holbrook, F. 1968. The faculty image of the academic librarian. *Southeastern Librarian* 18:174-193.

Holley, E. G. 1961. Effective librarian-faculty relationships. *Illinois Libraries* 43:731-741.

Ivey, R. T. 1994. Teaching faculty perceptions of academic librarians at Memphis State University. *College & Research Libraries* 55:69-82.

Johnson, S. 1990. Visiting librarians check out the issues. Read their lips: These conferees are concerned about a lot more than silence in the stacks. *Chicago Tribune*, 29 June.

Lanning, J. A. 1988. The library-faculty partnership in curriculum development. *College & Research Libraries News* 49:7-9.

Leigh, R. D., and K. W. Sewny. 1960. The popular image of the library and the librarian. *Library Journal* 85:2089-2091.

Logsdon, R. H. 1970. The librarian and the scholar: Eternal enemies. *Library Journal* 95:2871-2874.

Marchant, M. P. 1969. Faculty-librarian conflict. *Library Journal* 94:2886-2889.

Oberg, L. R., M. K. Schleiter, and M. V. Houten. 1989. Faculty perceptions of librarians at Albion College: Status, role, contribution, and contacts. *College & Research Libraries* 50:215-230.

Scherer, H. 1970. The faculty and the librarian. *The Library-College Journal* 3(4):37-43.

Tannenbaum, E. 1963. The librarian in the college novel. *College and Research Libraries* 24:248-250.

Looking Back to the Future:
Turn of the Last Century Librarians
Look Ahead to the Twentieth Century

Daniel Liestman

SUMMARY. This article reviews the American and British library literature of the late nineteenth and early twentieth centuries to see what librarians of this period expected libraries and librarianship to be like in the mid to late twentieth century. They expected librarians would be involved in a variety of services and outreach activities such as teaching children in the schools. These writers also anticipated a publishing glut with more books being printed than any library could acquire. Budgets, consequently, were expected to be tight. Though no one foresaw the computer, most expected technology to have an increasingly important role. Improvements in mechanical devices also meant a unified national catalog might be realized. This would be but the harbinger of other cooperative activities such as inter-library reference and lending. Writers also expected libraries would be imposing edifices. Finally, many forecast that librarians would become professionals. *[Article copies available for a fee from The Haworth Document Delivery Service: 1-800-HAWORTH. E-mail address: <docdelivery@haworthpress.com> Website: <http://www.HaworthPress. com> © 2002 by The Haworth Press, Inc. All rights reserved.]*

Daniel Liestman is Associate Director of Library Services, Florida Gulf Coast University, 10501 FGCU Boulevard South, Ft. Myers, FL 33965-6565 (E-mail: dliestma@ fgcu.edu).

[Haworth co-indexing entry note]: "Looking Back to the Future: Turn of the Last Century Librarians Look Ahead to the Twentieth Century." Liestman, Daniel. Co-published simultaneously in *The Reference Librarian* (The Haworth Information Press, an imprint of The Haworth Press, Inc.) No. 78, 2002, pp. 25-46; and: *The Image and Role of the Librarian* (ed: Wendi Arant, and Candace R. Benefiel) The Haworth Information Press, an imprint of The Haworth Press, Inc., 2002, pp. 25-46. Single or multiple copies of this article are available for a fee from The Haworth Document Delivery Service [1-800-HAWORTH, 9:00 a.m. - 5:00 p.m. (EST). E-mail address: docdelivery@haworthpress.com].

10.1300/J120v37n78_03

KEYWORDS. Forecasting, twentieth century–forecasts, libraries–aims and objectives, libraries–nineteenth century, library science–technological innovations, library science–professionalism

Let me . . . raise up my voice and, with humility, prophesy.

–Thompson 1889, 402

The turn of a century seems to mark a time for consideration over what has passed and of what is yet to transpire. As this present millennium dawned, predictions in both the general and professional literature considered what the next hundred or even thousand years would portend for librarians. There is, however, seldom an opportunity to see whether one's prognostications come to pass or not. This, of course, has advantages and disadvantages. In 1918, Arthur E. Bostwick, the head of the Saint Louis Public Library, speculated as to what library work would be like in thirty-two years. He noted, "If my forecast should turn out to be a failure no one can prove it until 1950 arrives, and then I shall not care" (Bostwick 1918, 51). Likewise, Ernest A. Savage saw little consequence if his 1903 predictions were in error. "If what I foretell does not come to pass, my screed will be forgotten in the Bloomsbury catacombs, since I shall not disturb it." But, the Sub-Librarian at Croydon Public Libraries in England added, "on the other hand there are advantages; for if I live to see my librarian of the future I shall not forget to drag my perpetration into the light of day, flourish it on his face and cry, 'Ah my friend: I saw you coming!'" (Savage 1903, 4).

While the current popular and professional literature of the late twentieth and early twenty-first centuries focuses on what the future holds, it is both illuminating and instructive to see what our professional forebearers saw as they looked ahead to the twentieth century. These visions do not always agree. They also vary in approach. Most of the predictions are vague, cautious, and safe–squarely predicated on the events of the recent past. Savage saw such predictions following in the tradition of H. G. Wells and Jules Verne, whom he complained sought to "build both charming and alarming edifices on the foundation of the ideas and tendencies of the present day"–this, he said, is the "scientific method of prophecy." He added that "like most scientific methods–for instance Dewey's Classification and Cutter's Alphabetical Tables–it sometimes leads to funny results." He advocated more imagination in predicting the librarian of the future (Savage 1903, 4). In this vein, George Watson

Cole, a protegee of Dewey, used considerable creativity in presenting his predictions as he took readers ahead one century on a fanciful journey to the Pennsylvania "State Bureau of Public Libraries" in October 1995 (Cole, "American Libraries," 1894, 3-10).

Savage's approbation aside, whatever approach is taken, these predictions about the last century are indicative of issues facing the profession then. The late nineteenth century was an exciting time for librarians. By 1848 William Frederick Poole, a student-librarian at Yale, published his first general periodical index. In 1876 the American Library Association was organized, the Commissioner of Education released his report on American libraries, and Melvil Dewey published the first edition of his decimal classification system. In Great Britain the Library Association was founded in 1877. That same year the Metropolitan Free Libraries Committee formed to improve free service in London. In 1879 the British Museum published the first national library catalog. By 1880 Andrew Carnegie was starting his philanthropic activities by donating his millions for the construction of free public libraries across the United States. It is no wonder that *Library Journal* founder Richard Rogers Bowker declared, "it will be the chief glory of the nineteenth century that it has organized knowledge. It is thus that the man of the future, who will have more to learn, will learn it more easily" (Bowker 1883, 247). In order to best understand the views of those who looked ahead to the past century, this paper will examine both library and popular American and British literature from as early as 1880 to as late as 1920 in terms of how librarians saw themselves as agents of change, anticipated changes within libraries, and advances in the profession.

In this earlier era of rapid change and growth the prophets drew a strong distinction between the librarians of the future, with whom they identified, and their hopelessly out-of-date predecessors. In an article in *Book Buyer*, clergyman Gerald Stanley Lee said a traditional librarian would have "a sort of brown, faded color," adding this "was the proper color for librarians" (Lee 1902, 56). Cole noted that the librarian of the eighteenth and early nineteenth centuries was a "collector *par excellence*" who "like the miser, gathered his treasures and hoarded them from unhallowed hands" (Cole, "American Libraries," 4). Others drew even less flattering characterizations. Looking to the past in 1903, Savage saw the old-fashioned librarian, deeply versed in bibliography and antiquarian lore being "short-sighted and bald with skin the color of old pages," and whose aim in life was "to grub up as many unnecessary facts as he can." This "ancient gentleman," he said needed to be replaced by one who will "not confine his attention to the 'getting and keeping of books' but who will take advantage of every labor saving device, in use by common business . . . to get the whole contents of a library under his control" (Savage 1903, 6).

Others tried to catch a glimpse of what librarians were becoming. In 1908 Herbert Quick of the Sioux City, Iowa Public Library saw contemporary librarians in a transitional phase. He declared, "The librarian of the twentieth century, who is to-day lying in his cradle," will have cataloging rules and other perplexing problems settled for him as a result of the "library conferences and micro-machia of these days." He concluded, "the librarian of today is a bridge builder. . . . He must use the materials of the past in building for the future" (Quick, 1908). Clearly, the British Museum's Principle Librarian, E. Maunde Thompson, was correct in noting the "halcyon days" when the librarian was "only a keeper of books" are "fled forever" (Thompson 1889, 410).

The future required a major attitudinal change in what the role of the librarian was to be. As Eric A. Peppiette of the Liverpool University Library observed in 1914, librarians were no longer mere caretakers of books, they now had a duty to bring people into contact with them "by every possible method" (Peppiette 1914, 17). Bowker saw the librarian being analogous to a missionary. "It is now the glory of the librarian that he is a liberator more than a keeper; he frees his books. The missionary relation of the librarian to his readers is one of the discoveries which the nineteenth century will hand along to the twentieth," he declared in 1883 (Bowker 1883, 248). Others picked up on this theme too. Nineteen years later, the Director of the New York Public Library, John Billings, concluded, librarians are "aggressive, energetic, and filled with the missionary and proselytizing spirit" (Billings 1902, 2). It is with some irony too, in 1919, Rabbi Emanuel Sternheim reiterated the same theme. In an address before the Northwest District of the Iowa Library Association he said, "librarians must be encouraged to be missionaries rather than collectors"–the librarian of tomorrow must create demand not just supply it (Sternheim 1919, 434).

The emerging role of public librarians as educators of the masses seemed to be a perfect opportunity to spread the gospel or good news of what libraries had to offer. From his fictive future vantage point of 1995 Cole observed, "Men wiser than their day and generation arose, who very naturally inquired 'of what value are these fine collections of books if they cannot be freely consulted by those desiring to do so?'" They then said, "let us establish libraries at the public expense, yes by taxation even, and throw them open freely to the people." He declared the future "is pre-eminently the age of the free public library" (Cole,

"American Libraries," 5, 3). Peppiette added "in his new sphere of activity the librarian naturally claims to fill a high place in the educational world." The library is to be "the university of the people, in which public taste for literature is guided, the desire for knowledge instilled, the work of research aided" (Peppiette, 17).

What was emerging was a new ethos of public service where the librarian or library assistants actively sought to engage the patron. The Reverend Lee facetiously pined for a time when a man such as himself with "a skittish or country mind will have a chance . . . to be alone with books," just books and "be permitted to browze [sic], unnoticed, bars all down, and risk his mind and roll himself, without turning over all of a sudden only to find a librarian's assistant standing there wondering at him, looking down to the bottom of his soul." He finally asked for "a little inconvenience, a little old-fashioned, happy inconvenience; a chance to gloat and take pains and love things with difficulties, a chance to go around the corners of one's knowledge, to make modest discoveries all by one's self" (Lee 1902, 57, 58).

Many anticipated that one of the chief objects of librarians' zeal would be school children. They saw the secret to future professional success in training children to become regular users of the library who, when they became older, would not depart from such habits. "The librarian, no less than the pedagogue, is a teacher," Quick noted, adding that in some respects the librarian's work is more important than that of the school. "The librarians are the tutor and mentors of adult life as well as childhood" (Quick 1908, 210). The exact nature of the much heralded public library-public school relationship was not "yet generally agreed upon by both librarians and teachers" Billings observed (Billings 1902, 1). Nevertheless, ideas abounded. Sternheim saw the local boards of education sharing with the cities the cost of providing, maintaining, and supervising suitable libraries for schools and the public. Cole foresaw that each library would keep in each school room a large number of books to supplement studies (Cole 1895, 10). Lewis Steiner, librarian at Baltimore's Enoch Pratt anticipated that the public library would also supply instructors with resources to guide and instruct pupils and consequently making the library's books of "incalculable value" (Steiner 1890, 46). British bibliographer Robert Alexander Peddie had a vision of librarians being even more involved. In an address before the Library Assistants Association in England, he spoke of a future where schoolmasters would teach and librarians would train children to read (Peddie 1901, 108). Still such partnering between librarians and teachers faced challenges. According to Billings, librarians would need to "supplement the defects and ignorance of each instructor in his own branch," but should also "treat them kindly and tactfully, recognizing it is not their fault they do not know as much as librarians" (Billings 1902, 2).

Assuming such cooperation could be attained, various benefits were to be achieved. Many saw the integration of school and public libraries as an opportunity to instill the values of life-long learning in children. Sternheim suggested libraries for elementary and high schools would provide children with reading for vocational needs, but also information on becoming good citizens. He even went so far as to suggest that the library must serve as a social institution "for if we can get our schools at a sufficiently high level we shall need no jails" (Sternheim 1919, 431, 433). While not as ambitious, A. L. Sawyer, President of the Board of Trustees of the Menominee Michigan Public Library, foresaw public libraries in schools reaching out to children in school and staying with them through life, and all the while reaching out to parents and neighbors who could not read or did not know English (Sawyer 1920, 1013). Sternheim further suggested libraries would encourage children to become participants in social democracy, adding, "if this happens the public library will become a potent factor in human life." Sawyer took this further, declaring librarians will "spread the influence of enlightening books" as a "patriotic work for the dissemination of the principles of true democracy," adding, libraries will "constitute a bulwark of defense against all insidious propaganda; a firm foundation for true Americanism" (Sawyer, 1013, 1017).

At the same time, Sternheim cautioned against overzealousness. He warned there had been too much made of censorship and the library of the future "must stand as an impregnable rock in the furtherance of the ideal of freedom of the printed page within every reasonable limit. . . . shall we therefore lessen the liberty of the dissent in order to legislate for indecency?" So with treason, he declared, "Liberty is a spirit not an abstraction. If a man is fundamentally disloyal, it matters very little whether he reads Howe or not. . . . The library must stand guardian over the inviolate rise of human liberty and all things that appertain to knowledge" (Sternheim 1919, 435).

Partnering with schools and an increased social role were only some of the anticipated changes. Based on the exceptional events of recent memory, librarians anticipated a century of extraordinary collection usage and growth lay before them. Arthur E. Bostwick, the head of the St. Louis Public Library, saw exponential growth of library usage. He pointed to the New York Public Library, which in 1898 circulated a million books. In 1918 when he spoke to the Saratoga Springs Conference of the American Library Association, New York Public was circulating ten million. "Does anybody believe," he asked, "that twenty years hence they will circulate one hundred million?" (Bostwick 1918, 52). Continued growth was projected for academic libraries too. In 1914, Oberlin College librarian, Azariah Smith Root pointed out that in 1875 Harvard and Yale were the only educational institutions in the U.S. with more than fifty-thousand volumes. By 1908 fifty-four academic libraries passed this mark. By 1941, he estimated, many major universities will have collections in excess of two million and will be spending $150,000/year on books (Root 1914, 811, 812).

The growth of publishing was expected to be one of the major issues of the twentieth century. As early as 1895, Frank Campbell, the noted British Museum bibliographer, complained, "the press continues to pour forth its tons of books, but we have no mill to digest them" (Campbell 1895, 34). For University of Minnesota law librarian Arthur Pulling, the future presented many hard choices. He asked, "what laws, periodicals, reports, textbooks, etc., shall be purchased and of what countries?" (Pulling 1915, 706). The rapid growth not only of collections, but of information in general provided other challenges. Campbell saw the rapid increase of scientific knowledge in 1894 as worrisome. He said that given "the fresh increase of scientific knowledge year by year, all *detailed* classification of scientific class-catalogues will periodically become obsolete and therefore most troublesome, if not altogether useless" (Campbell 1895, 39). Quick observed that while it once was true that almost any book was worth shelf room, this was not "universally true . . . the existing stock of books is so great and additions to it are so enormous that no ordinary library can possibly have them all. The librarian's duty becomes more and more the task of deciding what not to buy" (Quick 1908, 210-211).

He saw quality of collections as paramount and also cautioned against what he saw as a trend. The choice to be made is "between books which are mere books, and those which are literature," he said, adding, "but on you is placed the rather delicate task of refraining from buying some things because they ought not to be supplied, no matter what the demand." In popular literature he saw "all that is required is a sufficient degree of debasement to make possible the putting into novel size and book form of any filthy story which an hour's sojourn with the tramps gathered by the water tank and the nearest siding may furnish forth" (Quick 1908, 211). Beyond not catering to local prurient interests, others saw collections being defined in other ways.

Thompson suggested the acquisition of local literature as a desirable method of defining the local library. Such collections could form the core of a small library which might someday grow into a large library. "Free libraries established even in small country towns may be the centres around which will gather collections destined to be the pride of large cities, into which those same small towns may one day grow," he said. With an eye toward posterity he added, "it is from tiny facts and obscure names that local history and local topography are built up. In the sweepings of the lawyer's office there may exist priceless material for future antiquary . . . in the collection and preservation of local records the time has come for each town and district to seek its own." He concluded, "no person is more likely to take an intelligent interest in this accumulation of MS material than the local librarian" (Thompson 1889, 403-404). Beyond this, others saw collections changing in other ways. Bostwick saw the whole scope of the library's collection changing from books alone to printed matter of all kinds and records of other types such as manuscripts, pictures, slides, films, phonograph discs, and piano rolls (Bostwick 1918, 53).

Funding collections was expected to continue to be a challenge for librarians. Savage lamented, "It would be difficult to imagine the future library will ever be much richer than it is now, as people may not want to continue support to libraries through taxes" (Savage 1903, 5). In a *Popular Science* article Princeton reference librarian William Warner Bishop suggested that public libraries would increasingly be supported by taxes through legislative mandate (Bishop 1904, 138). Thompson also anticipated funding collections would continue to be an issue, but saw alternatives for establishing solid local collections. He lamented that "those who fund libraries hold parsimony as a virtue." He also offered the hope of donations of materials as a means of consoling future librarians. He noted, "that everywhere there are persons who, once they see a place established for the safe custody of antiquarian and other collections, will come forward and give" (Thompson 1889, 406).

In addition to growing collections, another major trend facing librarians was the advent of new technology. Savage said the librarian of the future would be particularly well informed in technical matters (Savage 1903, 5). Likewise Sir John Young Walker MacAlister, Librarian and Secretary, Royal Society of Medicine, declared that if the librarian of the future has mechanical abilities, "so much the better" (MacAlister 1898, 10). In 1914 Root anticipated labor saving devices would save the cataloger considerable time otherwise spent producing cards and allow her to specialize in cataloging certain fields such as European History

(Root 1914, 813). Steiner foresaw many applications of what he called "classification and mechanical appliances to assist in the details of administration." With "the best methods of doing this and that, the best forms of blanks wherewith accounts can be kept and statistics made practically available, how time and labor can be saved by such an invention," he declared (Steiner 1890, 45).

Emily Isabel Wade of the San Francisco Free Public Library addressed the impact of technology on access issues. For her the question was, "in what form and through what medium shall the catalogue be presented?" She wondered, "Shall it be that much abused old standby, the card catalogue, or is that to give place to those later contrivances the Leyden and Sacconi binders, or the Rudolph appliances?" For her the future was found in something beyond the traditional card catalog. Binders, she noted, were easy to handle and allowed for easy additions and updates. "Although superior in some ways" she observed they accumulated rapidly and take up considerable space. Another problem is that, as with the card catalogue, the "direct contact with the hands of a not too clean public, they are liable to become gradually unfit to be used" and eventually must be replaced by new ones–which requires recopying–"a fruitful source of errors." For her, the catalog of the future was to be found in the Rudolph Indexer. This device had the advantage of being under glass and displaying six pages at a time. The "small exertion of turning a crank, economizes the time and consequently much of the nerve power of the searcher." Still, she acknowledged, it was not perfect as the insertions had to be placed carefully in the Indexer and needed to be done by "skilled laborers." If the Indexer was filled too full there would be a "piled heap on the bottom of the box. . . . But allowing for all these shortcomings, it is the most satisfactory contrivance that has been produced thus far" (Wade 1895, 21).

Wade also saw new ways in which cards could actually be produced too. For her the answer was the linotype (Wade 1895, 22). Such a machine offered long term benefits as the life of the type was estimated at fifty-thousand impressions. In fact she reported there was a newly patented copper faced type which was estimated to last a century (Wade 1895, 23). The linotype promised to bring the advantages of mass production to the catalog making the holdings available to the masses. "A guide which brings the contents of the library before the busy public in the simplest, most easy comprehended manner, is the best for all practical purposes," she said, adding that with the linotype, catalogs in the future will not be "the almost unattainable luxury which they are at present" (Wade 1895, 24).

Wade also suggested the type-bars could be stored, which would encourage the "much-discussed idea of centralization in cataloging" (Wade, 23). As most libraries are composed of much the same works, Wade posited, a certain number should be able to get together and decide on the same classification scheme, a "Central Bureau" could furnish the required slips to be inserted in the catalog, and a printed catalog could be produced the same way too (Wade 1895, 23). As centralized cataloging became more of a reality, Caroline Wandell suggested utilization of another recent invention. The present, she said is "the most opportune time for adopting the typewriter for cataloging purposes." She said, the headings can be written so neatly that "to the casual observer the difference can hardly be noticed" (Wandell 1902, 268).

Still, not all were so taken with things mechanical. In 1901, Frederick M. Crunden, founder of the St. Louis Public Library and former ALA President, warned that technical matters and devices threatened to overrun the essence of the profession. "The mechanics of librarianship must not be allowed to usurp the place of its spirit," he cried. "Methods count for less than culture; and the qualities essential to the highest success are enthusiasm, sympathy, tact, and self-devotion" (Crunden 1901, 141). Earlier MacAlister wondered what the impact of technology would be on librarianship. "A librarian who wants to distinguish himself is driven to mechanical inventions designed to save either the time of himself or his readers," he observed, adding,

> My critics will tell you that the more time saving apparatus is used is more time the librarian will have to cultivate his intellect and discourse with his readers on the beauties of Browning or Byron. But is the time saved by mechanism used in this excellent way? I am afraid not. The taste for such things grows on what it feeds, and the librarian who has invented an appliance for supplying his readers with books (they would rather not have) by the means of an automatic ticket-in-the-slot machine will not be happy, or spend anytime in reading Browning, until he has invented one which will by the touching of a button, shoot the book into the reader's home, and so save the busy librarian the time lost in opening the library door. Master craftsmen tell us that an excess of time-saving machinery and consequent specialization of labor deadens the intellects of the workers. . . . And so I think we should do well to rest content for a while with our present mechanical achievement and devote the time thus saved to the polishing up of our own intellectual armoury–in too many cases grown rusty for want of use. (MacAlister 1898, 10)

In spite of such misgivings, technology also lent itself to another new trend in cataloging–centralization and inter-library cooperation in cataloging and other services. Such moves were seen as increasing efficiency and reducing redundancy. William Howard Brett, Director of the Cleveland Public Library, wrote an article in *The Dial* declaring "effective cooperation" to be the most important characteristic of modern library enterprises (Brett 1903, 75). Cole stated the preparation and printing of a catalog is a source of great expense for individual libraries. The time and labor involved in preparing a catalog is "simply appalling" (Cole, "Cataloging in the Future," 24). Savage added, "The public will not stand for the wasteful method of cataloging the same books a couple of hundred times at a couple hundred centres" (Savage 1903, 5). Billings took a colder analysis, noting that with cataloging consolidated, "most libraries could dismiss their cataloguers and one half the money now used for salaries could be used for buying more books" (Billings 1902, 4).

Others saw the advantages to researchers if libraries cooperated to create a unified catalog. No one can be certain of obtaining all the information desired on a particular topic without going in many different directions–"an impossible task" said Campbell declaring, "it remains therefore to remedy this great evil!" (Campbell 1895, 41). Toward that end, the Library of Congress proposed in 1901 to furnish printed cards to all American libraries for the cost of producing them. Some years later, Pulling took this a step further, calling for a catalog which would furnish "references to libraries where each book might be found," as it was clear that no library could own everything (Pulling 1915, 708). Co-operation in cataloging was seen as an answer to a number of problems. Not only was it seen as benefitting smaller libraries, but larger central ones too. Billings said co-operation should not be just top down. Smaller libraries had a responsibility to "send copies of all local non-copyrighted materials including municipal reports and documents to the Library of Congress" (Billings 1902, 3).

Assuming librarians a century later would implement such trends and partake in this efficient new world, George Cole took a fanciful futuristic journey to the Pennsylvania "State Bureau of Public Libraries" in October A.D. 1995 to catch a glimpse of such a brave new world one hundred years hence. The State Bureau controlled all the libraries in the state–initially control and supervision was just of public libraries, but others, "seeing the great advantage to be derived by being connected with the Bureau petitioned the state's General Assembly to pass a law allowing them to be included under the Bureau's authority." The Bureau library was made up of "bibliographies, catalogues, biographies, works of literary history and criticism, and those on library methods and management." It also contained a completed copy of Sabin from A-Z with eight to ten supplementary volumes, one hundred-nineteen volumes of *Library Journal*, of which volumes earlier than 1950 were seldom consulted except for historical purposes as the "methods in vogue in libraries previous to that date were now considered so clumsy as to be wholly impractical." Cole learned of a "great advance" in the middle of the twentieth century when the movement to put all libraries under the control of the general government had been proposed and adopted. The National Bureau of Public Libraries was the foremost authority on all questions pertaining to bibliography and library administration. The state commissioners, he said, are elected by the people to ten year terms and elect one of their own from the National Council to serve as the National Commissioner. The Council is responsible for deciding all issues of library methodology and management. By about 1950, Cole learned, the National Council adopted a uniform classification system. Pennsylvania, like all the other fifty-six states, fell in line and the State Commissioner formed a staff of expert catalogers and classifiers to implement the code of rules and system of classification adopted by the Council. Pennsylvania's largest library initially undertook this project, at the state's expense. Catalogued entries were "electrotyped," with a single plate for each entry, and printed cards sent to each library in the state. As each library found it owned an identical edition of the book so cataloged, it added the cards and began to create a new catalog. Unused cards were returned to the Bureau and records were kept on which cards were retained by which libraries. When the first library was done the next in size went through the same process. This continued until every library in the state had been cataloged. In the late twentieth century Cole discovered, libraries no longer had to "employ a skilled cataloger and staff to assist him as was done during the comparatively unenlightened days of the nineteenth century." Instead, the work was now done by the "most highly trained corps of catalogers ever gathered in the state, and in a far more thorough manner than any librarian had heretofore ever had the courage or authority to do it." By 1987 the libraries of all the states were cataloged and the aggregate mass of cards formed a most impressive bibliography. At this same time, Congress passed laws requiring every printer and publisher to forward to his state bureau an advance copy of every work for official cataloging and classification. The "publisher was compelled to issue all necessary cards, printed according to fixed rules, upon standard sized cards which must be furnished to the purchaser of the work." This system was eventually adopted by "all enlightened countries" and a system of international exchange of publications and cataloging resulted (Cole, "American Libraries," 8, 9).

While Cole's vision may strike some as being overly regulated, he was not alone. Bishop foresaw state library commissions becoming involved in the inspection of local libraries as a means to improve their efficiency (Bishop 1904, 138). These visions pale in comparison to Campbell who said the work of national bibliography can alone be satisfactorily performed by the states and the following auxiliary societies created to carry out this work: a society for the establishment of compulsory book registration, a society for the investigation of subject-classification, a compilers of periodical special bibliographies society, a society to investigate the bibliography of periodical literature, an index society, an international bibliographic society, an official state papers/bibliographical society, and a county and municipal official literature society (Campbell 1895, 46-47)!

Cole also touched on a key issue when he suggested all enlightened countries participated in such a system–a comprehensive international bibliography. Some librarians, such as Bowker suggested that once the British Museum printed catalog became a fact, the "utopian universal catalogue" becomes a certainty. He saw that a second alphabet of books in other libraries would be started before the nineteenth century closed, and the librarian of the twentieth century "has only to roll them into one, to insert from time to time the discoveries that still must be made and use the methods we are already providing for the easy cataloging of the world's accessions" (Bowker 1883, 249).

Not all were convinced of the advantages of centralization and cooperative cataloging. MacAlister complained that akin to "mechanicalism" is the "loftier in aim [and] almost equally dangerous . . . exaggerated value attached by many to co-operative work." He found "one gigantic universal catalogue of cards, one gigantic universal index of knowledge, also on cards" disconcerting. The sheer size of any such catalog, MacAlister feared would "overwhelm you by their unwieldy immensity; the references to John Smith alone, and his achievement in the regions of theology or of crime would fill the British Museum, and would make it necessary to found a college of John Smith specialism" (MacAlister 1898, 11). He also feared such centralization would have a countervailing effect on the budding professional status of librarianship. "Such a central bureau of 'bibliology' with a score of consulting experts on library economy could organize all the libraries in the British Empire in five years and would find a staff of junior clerks at 20 shilling a week each quite adequate for the work of the library . . . and where should we be?" he asked (MacAlister 1898, 11). Still others did not view this as a problem. Savage acknowledged "co-operation will remove from the librarian's shoulders some important parts of the duties he now does," but saw this as an opportunity to have more time to work with the public (Savage 1903, 5).

In spite of such misgivings, inter-library cooperation was seen as something applicable to a variety of other endeavors too. Root saw that libraries constantly receive gifts which are duplicates and at the same time other libraries have or receive incomplete runs. Rather than sell them to a second hand dealer for a mere fraction of their real monetary value, other libraries could buy them "at price five to ten times higher than what the dealer pays." Simple author title lists, easily duplicated and sent out freely, would serve all libraries and allow the selling library to make some money (Root 1914, 814). An unsigned *Outlook* article even suggested that rare and valuable manuscripts should be reproduced by "certain photographic processes" to ensure their posterity and make them available to scholars overseas. To copy many of the significant documents in European libraries for the benefit of American researchers the author estimated it would cost twenty-five thousand dollars ("Increase of Library Influence" 1904, 448).

Cooperation could extend to reference work as well. "Every day reference departments prepare lists of books, finding material upon all sorts of out of the way and unusual subjects or working out some perplexing problem as to authorship," Root observed. To a certain extent the same questions would arise in other libraries too. He suggested compiling and duplicating such queries and sending them to other libraries to be located in a vertical file for quick future reference. "The cost of duplicating and postage would be well worth it," he added (Root 1914, 814).

In addition Cole saw that books were to be freely loaned from one library to another for brief periods with low postal rate facilitating such an exchange (Cole, "American Libraries," 9). By the turn of the twentieth century larger libraries had already taken the lead in sharing resources among themselves. Boston Public, for example, loaned 461 titles to other libraries in 1901 (Brett 1903, 77). Likewise, Bostwick saw "One of our greatest opportunities lies before us in the inter-library loan. It knocks at our door, but we do not heed it because in this respect we have not begun yet to think nationally." In the future he said reader's cards will be used interchangeably and interlibrary loans will take place easily and often (Bostwick 1918, 55). Indeed Brett saw that, "it is not an altogether improbable dream that the time will come when the student in any part of the country may have from any collection, however remote, the free use at his own fireside of any book which he may need for an important and worthy purpose" (Brett 1903, 77). Taking this idea one step further, Bostwick saw that library assistants will also be exchanged freely to facilitate better teamwork between libraries (Bostwick 1918, 56).

Billings saw libraries cooperating in other ways too. If selection were carried out among library cooperatives, he saw that book publishers would want to cooperate with libraries in determining what types of literature are most in demand. A committee of librarians would suggest subjects and writers, read manuscripts, and indicate which illustrations would boost sales. From there, he foresaw, libraries could take up selling these books which had been produced especially for public libraries (Billings 1902, 4). As for rare works, Cole saw they were to be reproduced by facsimile process at reasonable rates thereby easing the demand for them (Cole, "American Libraries," 10).

While centralization was seen as useful for cataloging and other departments, there was considerable expectation that service points would be diversified with branch or special libraries to meet the needs of specific groups of patrons. Brett envisioned a central library which would have many "branches and stations" "placed to bring books within reasonable distance of all parts of the city" (Brett 1900, 10). In academic libraries such an approach was also advocated. Benjamin Rand, the Canadian-born founder of the Emerson Hall philosophy library at Harvard, suggested that a specialized library such as was found at the University's prestigious law school was successful because it was administered by subject experts in the department. He suggested that a library, like any good laboratory, does well only when conducted by "those who give their lives to the task, and never by mere general supervision" as would occur with general library administration. Nevertheless, he still saw a need for a central library which would comprise a general collection of books of equal value to the whole university; special collections which could not be justifiably placed in any one department; "live books" in current use; general reports, records, and documents of interest to the general community as well as general reading rooms. Administrative work would also be one of the most important functions of the central library where the best methods of delivery, cataloging, shelving, ordering, and organization would occur. Departmental libraries could occur in separate buildings or in the central library (Rand 1907, 263).

Such suggestions then beg the question as to what the libraries of the twentieth century were expected to look like. It was widely agreed that librarians would work in imposing yet functional edifices. In his visit to the future, Cole discovered the State Bureau Library recently moved from its quarters in the capitol "for want of room" to "a fine large building which had been specially erected for its use" (Cole, "American Libraries," 8). Brett, a recognized expert on library design, saw a central "great reference library" with architecture "worthy of the important role it fills in civic life, with provision made for public comfort" (Brett 1900, 10). Bowker summarized, "whether the perfect library of the future shall be one great hall, walled with books, with its effective appeal to the imagination, and its artistic enticement to readers, its difficulties of length and distance overcome by mechanical devices for the delivery of books; or Prof. Winsor's stack-house . . . ; or the circular library with its radial alcoves, inviting readers to the open shelves under the all controlling vision of the librarian at the center" or a cellular plan, "providing for growth by rooms each of which may be a specialized library, within distance of a common focus remained to be seen" (Bowker 1883, 249). Billings and Brett both suggested that in order to meet the needs of future patrons, public libraries could be made into social centers and become substitutes for saloons. These would not only provide quiet study space and lecture rooms, but a drafting room with architecture books, and a darkroom for the photographer as well as rooms for game playing, smoking, and billiards, and even public baths in the basement (Billings 1902, 5; Brett 1900, 9).

Regardless of where librarians worked, another aspect of the future was the professionalization of librarianship. A Miss M. Gilbert, writing in *The Library Assistant* lamented that "too often the term librarian is lightly used" and is given to "an official who is placed in charge of a collection" and who possesses only "meager knowledge of their contents and less of the profession to which he purports to belong" (Gilbert, 28). Professionalization offered the hope for respect. Anyone looking over the past fifty years of librarianship, Philadelphia librarian Margaret Reed said, "with generous sympathy will realize the shortcomings of the profession are due to crushing poverty of the institutions, the librarians, and their assistants and the belittling influences of committees, councils, boards, and the public." She concluded that "instead of being members of the glorious calling of literature we were little more than scullions" (Reed, 40-41). In England, Savage foresaw that the mark of the professional would be certification by the Library Association (Savage, 4). In the future United States, Bostwick said there would be official certification and inspection of systems of service, noting such standardization was on the increase and was expected to be enforced with greater strictness. He also saw that professionalism as symptom of a great many things–of achievement, consciousness of it, and pride in it and also of a desire to do teamwork and to maintain standards, and to make sure that one's work is to be carried on and advanced by worthy successors (Bostwick 1918, 51).

As a professional, the librarian would be proactive in meeting constituents. Savage saw that the librarian "needs to be in the intellectual swim"–that is being involved in local societies and clubs not to poke books in their faces but just to represent the library. He noted, lecturing will be one of his most important duties–not general lectures which have no place in library work but "the purely and unashamedly advertising and expository talks. He will advertise the books by talking round them to students and over and over again demonstrate the value of catalogues and library printed aids." In short, the librarian would be able to speak and lecture well in "nearly every sort of society existing in the appallingly democratic future" (Savage 1903, 5). Bostwick sounded another sour note. Although he foresaw the desirability of library work as a profession will be greatly increased–"it will not necessarily pay very much better" (Bostwick, 56).

Professionalism was an outcome of systematic library school training. Professional education was seen as producing qualified librarians and enabling the professionalization of librarianship. Qualification through education, Gilbert declared, "is not just desirable, it is imperative" (Gilbert 1920, 27). Moreover, professional education was seen as one of the hallmarks of other professions and a model librarians sought to emulate. Although Dewey had already started his Library School, there was still discussion as to what the nature of professional education should entail and how closely it should emulate other models. "All of us would like to see librarianship raised and developed into a profession," MacAlister said. "The learned professions (to be regarded as one of which is our aspiration) are recruited by men who, after enjoying a liberal education, deliberately, from their own bent or by the advice of their friends, choose a profession, and then begin a special course of training lasting about five years" (MacAlister, 11). Gilbert noted that just as physicians no longer "walk" the hospital to learn medicine, librarians should be trained as well to meet the rigors of an increasingly demanding profession. What is soon coming she said is the "placing of Librarianship as a *profession*, upon a university basis." With the founding of a School of Librarianship at the University of London, she said that the need for qualification other than by experience has been recognized by authorities outside the profession. This acknowledgment "marks the evolution of librarianship from the trades to the ranks of the professions" (Gilbert, 26, 28).

With professionalism would also come specialization. Bostwick saw a distinction between public and university library work in library school curricula (Bostwick 1918, 54). Peppiette observed, only a few decades ago the librarian was "all-embracing in his duties." What he saw was an increasingly diversified field with "specialists in many departments–in cataloging, classification, juvenile work and reference work–to mention only a few" (Peppiette, 17). Gilbert suggested librarians needed to "specialize beyond classification and cataloging" and other technical aspects of librarianship. She said the librarian needed to develop expertise in aspects of literature and local history and many more which may be of interest (Gilbert 1920, 29). Steiner expressed concerns about over-specialization. He advised, the line of study to be taken by librarians should be to be able to advise, aid, and assist. The librarian may have his own areas of special study, but he should not prosecute them to the point of dereliction of his other duties (Steiner 1890, 44). At the same time Savage saw the librarian as having to have a broadly based education. The ideal librarian, he said, "will know besides bibliography, and the technique of his craft," at least two foreign languages, history, literature, and some sociology (Savage 1903, 6).

Beyond whatever education was required, future librarians and head librarians, in particular, were seen as needing a number of special innate characteristics and life experiences in order to be successful. The librarian must "be a smart business man, with a faculty for organization," said MacAlister (MacAlister 1898, 10). Sawyer suggested the librarian of the future should be highly educated and specially trained, because "not only executive capacity in directing the work of the staff, but organizing capacity, ability to meet, discern and deal with every make up of human nature is required and not the least an extensive knowledge of books, and the methods of selection thereof." He added that the other requisite was that "every librarian and every member of the staff should be in the work because of the love thereof" (Sawyer 1920, 1014). ALA President Herbert Putnam said the modern librarian must be informed not only to the book, but to the reader: "he must understand him and what actuates him." In addition, he must have wide familiarity with current events "gained not by formal education but by travel and varied social contacts, and this goes not just for the Librarian-in-chief but the entire 'interpreting staff" who must also have temperament and instinct for service" (Putnam, 89).

To conclude, Gilbert noted, the future is a topic "upon which most people can be very eloquent and about which nobody knows anything" (Gilbert 1920, 25). On one hand, she was right. None of the literature reviewed saw clearly the use of computers or the World Wide Web, with the possible exception of MacAlister's labor saving mechanism. Though there were certainly expectations that new mechanical devices would increase the efficiency of librarians. Nor were women seen as having a role in the profession until World War I. In most of the articles written prior to 1914 in both the U.S. and England, the librarian is referred to using the masculine pronoun, "he." One notable exception is MacAlister who in 1898, declared, "the profession will appeal to both men and women who like to work among and through books and with and through people" (MacAlister 1898, 10). Other issues pertaining to diversity were all but ignored. At the same time, these glimpses into the future from a century ago are not all that far from reality. The role of technology and the functionalities of public service, the essence of professional education are still issues of significance.

It is also clear that the majority of librarians in this time were highly optimistic about the future of the profession and the positive nature of progress. It was time to reach out and serve new constituencies in a variety of exciting and innovative ways. There was no perceived fear of becoming antiquated–though there were expectations that catalogers and classifiers would be less needed. Nor was there indication of the legal constraints ranging from filtering to copyright impacting the profession today. Intellectual freedom was an issue, but only in the sense that librarians needed to police themselves better in selecting literature rather than just fiction. Quick concluded, "the great book can wait. If it comes knocking at your doors year after year let it in. If it stays in the muck heap at the first rejection you may be sure that is the proper place for it" (Quick 1908, 211).

At the same time librarians were not pollyanna-ish about their future either. Few would argue with Bowker in 1883 when he said the "two great needs" of the twentieth century will be, "more money for books and more adequate pay for the librarian" (Bowker 1883, 250). Another underlying theme is that librarians were seen as struggling for respect. Reed spoke of the ongoing "belittling influences of committees, councils, boards, and the public" (Reed 1920, 41).

What pessimism existed in the literature was in response to the changes already ongoing with librarians. An unsigned article in *Scribner's* entitled "The Imperfect Librarian," lamented the modernism of the efficient but sterile approach to librarianship in which there were "so many mechanical details to be attended to in a well-managed modern library" as typified by the "cold glance of the young woman in shirt-waist and eye-glasses who, at the circulating desk is handling books with up-to-the minute movements that indicate this is no world to moon in." This author regretted there were few in the profession who were able to infuse it with the aroma of the psychic element to be found in the pure pleasure of browsing ("The Imperfect Librarian" 1900, 252).

For the librarians of the nineteenth and early twentieth centuries the future offered both change and consistency. Bostwick noted this presciently in 1918 when he wrote,

> the flier that reaches New York is the same train that left Chicago; its passengers have not greatly changed, and yet its environment is wholly different, so that the outlook of those within it has totally altered. It is in some such fashion that the library of 1950 will differ from that of today. It will be the same institution with the same staff, but it will have traveled far on the rails of time. Its environment, its outlook will be different, and in response to that variation it must need to do different things and render a different service. May its motive power never fail, its machinery be kept well oiled, and the crew maintain their strength, intelligence and sanity! (Bostwick, 57)

Bowker concluded that the "present work is to bear its results in the future, in the sense of the immortality of influence that comes of passing along the torch from generation to generation. The librarian of the twentieth century, for whom we are working, ought to be much better and do much better than his illustrious predecessors" (Bowker, 250).

May the same be said of us.

WORKS CITED

Bishop, William Warner. "A Decade of Library Progress in America." *Popular Science* 66 (December 1904): 131-138.

Billings, John S. "Some Library Problems of To-morrow: Address of the President." *Library Journal* 27 (December 1902): 1-9.

Bostwick, Arthur E. "The Future of Library Work." *Bulletin of the American Library Association* 12 (September 1918): 50-57.

Bowker, R. R. "The Work of the Nineteenth-Century Librarian for the Librarian of the Twentieth." *Library Journal* 8 (September-October, 1883): 247-250.

Brett, William Howard. "Modern Library Enterprises." *The Dial* 34 (February 1, 1903): 75-77.

Brett, W. H. "The Public Library of the Future." *Library Journal* 25 (February 1900): 69-70.

Cole, George Watson. "American Libraries; Their Past Present and Future." *Occasional Papers of the Pennsylvania Library Club* (no. 3) 1895, pp. 3-10.

Cole, George Watson. "Cataloging in the Future." *Library Journal* 20 (December 1895): 24.

Campbell, Frank. "The Bibliography of the Future," *The Library*, Series I vol. 7 (1895): 33-48.

Crunden, F. M. "What Is the Public Library For?" *Library Journal* 26 (March 1901): 141.

Gilbert, Miss M. "Librarianship of the Future." *The Library Assistant* 262 (April 1920): 25-29.

"The Imperfect Librarian." *Scribner's* 27 (February 1900): 252.

"Increase of Library Influence." *The Outlook* 76 (February 20, 1904): 447-448.

Lee, Gerald Stanley. "Wanted: An Old fashioned Librarian." *Book Buyer* 25 (August 1902): 55-58.

MacAlister, J. Y. W. "Some Tendencies of Modern Librarianship." *Transactions and Proceedings of the Second International Library Conference.* (London: The Conference, 1898): 9-12.

Peddie, R. A. "The May Meeting: Past, Present and Future of Public Libraries." *The Library Assistant* 3 (June 1902): 107-109.

Peppiette, Eric A. "Some Reflections on Modern Librarianship." *The Library Assistant* 14 (February 1917): 16-21.

Pulling, Arthur C. "The Law Library of the Future." *Library Journal* 40 (October 1915): 704-713.

Putnam, Herbert. "Are You a Modern Librarian?" *Library Occurrent* 4 (January 1916): 89-90.

Quick, Herbert. "The Librarian of Today." *Iowa Library Quarterly* 5 (April-May-June 1908): 210-211.

Rand, Benjamin. "The Future of the University Library." *The Nation* 84 (March 21, 1907): 263.

Reed, Margaret. "The Past, The Present, and the Future." *The Librarian* 10 (1920): 40-41.

Root, Azariah S. "The Future Development of College and University Libraries." *Library Journal* 39 (November 1914): 811-823.

Savage, Ernest A. "The Librarian of the Future." *The Library World* 6 (July 1903): 4-7.

Sawyer, A. L. "The Model Library of the Future." *Library Journal* 45 (December 15, 1920): 1013-1017.

Steiner, Lewis H. "The Future of the Free Public Library." *Library Journal* 15 (December 1890): 44-47.

Sternheim, Emanuel. "The Public Library of Tomorrow." *Library Journal* 44 (July 1919): 429-436.

Thompson, E. Maunde. "Some Hints on the Future of Free Libraries." *The Library* 1 (1889): 402-410.

Wade, Emily Isabel. "Cataloging in the Future." *Library Journal* 20 (December 1895): 21-24.

Wandell, Caroline. "The Typewriter for Card Catalogs." *Library Journal* 22 (May 1902): 268.

CULTURAL IMAGES

Jungian/Myers-Briggs Personality Types of Librarians in Films

Jeanine Williamson

SUMMARY. The Myers-Briggs personality typology provides a useful tool for characterizing the probable personality types of librarians portrayed in films. In this study, the probable personality types of librarians in 28 films are determined. Then comparisons with the personality types reported in Scherdin (1994) are made. Sex roles and stereotyping are revealed by these comparisons and are discussed. *[Article copies available for a fee from The Haworth Document Delivery Service: 1-800-HAWORTH. E-mail address: <docdelivery@haworthpress.com> Website: <http://www. HaworthPress.com> © 2002 by The Haworth Press, Inc. All rights reserved.]*

KEYWORDS. Personality, image, librarians in films

Jeanine Williamson is Engineering Reference Librarian, Hodges Library, University of Tennessee, Knoxville, TN 37995-1000 (E-mail: jwilliamson@utk.edu).

[Haworth co-indexing entry note]: "Jungian/Myers-Briggs Personality Types of Librarians in Films." Williamson. Jeanine. Co-published simultaneously in *The Reference Librarian* (The Haworth Information Press, an imprint of The Haworth Press, Inc.) No. 78, 2002, pp. 47-59; and: *The Image and Role of the Librarian* (ed: Wendi Arant, and Candace R. Benefiel) The Haworth Information Press, an imprint of The Haworth Press, Inc., 2002, pp. 47-59. Single or multiple copies of this article are available for a fee from The Haworth Document Delivery Service [1-800-HAWORTH. 9:00 a.m. - 5:00 p.m. (EST). E-mail address: docdelivery@ haworthpress.com].

10.1300/J120v37n78_04

INTRODUCTION

Personality may be thought of as giving information about a person, her likes and dislikes, and perhaps her positive and negative characteristics. Film makers are skilled depictors of personality, knowing that portraying characters with particular personality characteristics will convey familiar information to viewers who are experienced with stereotypes and with interacting with different kinds of people. This is particularly true of portrayals of librarians in films, in which librarians are given personality characteristics that reinforce positive and negative stereotypes. Examples include the stereotype of the helpful librarian with strong inner values, and that of the restrictive, rule-enforcing librarian. A system of personality typology originated by Swiss psychiatrist Carl G. Jung (1875-1961), and further developed by Katharine Cook Briggs and Isabel Briggs Myers, is useful for classifying the personalities that filmmakers portray. The Jungian/Myers-Briggs system organizes information associated with 16 personality types and makes this information coherent with underlying theory. This paper will briefly describe Jungian/Myers-Briggs personality theory and then give the results of applying the typology to 28 films in which librarians are characters. The results will be compared with actual personality types of librarians as reported in Scherdin (1994), and stereotypes and sex roles will be pointed out.

Background

Carl G. Jung described his theory of personality types in *Psychological Types* (1971). Jung identified two orientations of energy, extraversion (a direction of energy primarily towards the outside world), and introversion (a direction of energy primarily towards inner reflection), which he called *attitudes*. He also theorized from his extensive observations of people that there are also four *functions* arranged into two dichotomies:[1] Sensation vs. Intuition (both are Perceiving functions that take in information); and Thinking vs. Feeling (both are Judging functions that organize information and come to conclusions about it). Jung described the eight types resulting from the combination of Introversion or Extraversion with Sensation, Intuition, Thinking, or Feeling, resulting in a most preferred function. Thus, a person whose dominant function was Introverted Sensation, would typically enjoy concentrating on inner representations of facts and past experiences (internalized information taken in through the senses), because she would prefer to use Sensation in an introverted manner, rather than any other function.

Myers and Briggs modified Jung's typology to flesh out theoretical points he had not fully developed, and also succeeded in making it more accessible. Instead of Sensation, Myers and Briggs used the term Sensing, a preference for focusing on what can be perceived by the senses. Intuition was defined as a preference for focusing on perceiving patterns and interrelationships. Thinking was defined as preferring to base conclusions on logical analysis in an objective, detached manner. Feeling was defined as preferring to base conclusions on personal or social values in an understanding, harmonizing manner (Myers, McCaulley, Quenk, Hammer, 1998). The Myers-Briggs typology represents each of 16 types with four letters: I or E (Introversion versus Extraversion), S or N (Sensing or Intuition), T or F (Thinking or Feeling), and J or P (Judging or Perceiving). Thus each Myers-Briggs "formula" tells a person's preferred energy orientation, her preferred information-receiving function, her preferred decision-making function, and whether she prefers to act in the outside world in a Judging or Perceiving manner. Myers and Briggs defined the Judging orientation to the outside world as preferring decisiveness and closure in one's outer dealings. They defined the Perceiving orientation to the outside world as preferring flexibility and spontaneity in one's outer dealings.

There are other theoretical matters that could be discussed, but it is sufficient to note that the Jungian/Myers-Briggs typology has produced descriptions of 16 personality types (widely popularized through the extensive use of the Myers-Briggs Type Indicator®), whose characteristics relate to an attitude (I/E), a perceiving function (S/N), a judging function (T/F), and a preferred orientation to the outside world (J/P). An advantage of the typology was stated by Isabel Briggs Myers: "The merit of the theory presented here is that it enables us to expect specific personality differences in particular people and to cope with the people and the differences in a constructive way. Briefly, the theory is that much seemingly chance variation in human behavior is not due to chance; it is in fact the logical result of a few basic, observable differences in mental functioning" (Briggs Myers 1990, 1).

An interesting research question in light of the accepted fact that films employ stereotypes from popular culture is whether film stereotypes can be characterized in terms of personality types. If characters of only a few personality types are used to depict a profession such as librarianship, this would seem to indicate that these personality types represent popularly held stereotypes. Since research has been done on librarians' actual personality types (Scherdin 1994), comparison of film personality stereotypes with real personality type frequencies is possible.

METHODS

A convenience sample of 28 films was selected from the Librarians in Film Bibliography (Raish 2000) that were readily available in local libraries and video stores. The researcher viewed each film and took notes about the librarian characters' personality characteristics. Best guesses of the characters' types were made based on knowledge from previous study of Myers-Briggs descriptions of the 16 types. As an additional check, the researcher tried to determine whether the librarian character extraverted Feeling, or displayed Feeling in the outside world, (e.g., attempted to connect with others, tried to please others, was charming, was physically expressive, and praised or blamed others) (Tieger and Baron-Tieger 1998). Types which extravert Feeling include ISFJ, ESFJ, INFJ, ENFJ, ENTP, ESTP, ISTP, INTP. If a character seemed to extravert Feeling, this was helpful in either narrowing down his or her type or providing a confirmation of a proposed type assignment.

In most of the films librarian-characters had major roles, and there was extensive information available to make a best guess about personality type. In a few, however (*Big Sleep, Blade, Scream 3, Somewhere in Time*, and *With Honors*), the librarian was only shown briefly, and the hypothesis about type was based on less evidence.

RESULTS

Overrepresented and Underrepresented Types

Thirty-one librarian characters were characterized as to type from the 28 films. In some films there were more than one librarian character. The Appendix shows selected evidence used to determine characters' types. The frequencies of the 16 Myers-Briggs types were calculated and compared with type distributions of librarians reported in Scherdin (1994). Table 1 gives the frequencies of the 16 Myers-Briggs personality types in the film sampled, and below each type frequency it gives the ratio of this type frequency to the type frequency among real librarians.

TABLE 1. Personality Types of Librarians in Films Compared with Real Librarians

Type Frequency Type Frequency/ Type Frequency among real librarians			
ISTJ n = 5 .16 .78	ISFJ n = 10 .32 3.95	INFJ n = 1 .03 .46	INTJ n = 2 .06 .52
ISTP n = 0 0 0	ISFP n = 3 .10 5.88	INFP n = 4 .13 1.78	INTP n = 0 0 0
ESTP n = 2 .06 5.45	ESFP n = 0 0 0	ENFP n = 1 .03 .5	ENTP n = 1 .03 .51
ESTJ n = 1 .03 .49	ESFJ n = 1 .03 .73	ENFJ n = 0 0 0	ENTJ n = 0 0 0

The ratios of type frequencies to type frequencies of real librarians indicate whether types are overrepresented or underrepresented. Types having ratios over 1.0 may be considered overrepresented. Overrepresented types in the films sampled include ISFJ, ISFP, INFP, ESTP. Ratios less than 1.0 indicate underrepresented types. Underrepresented types include ISTJ, INFJ, INTJ, ISTP, INTP, ESFP, ENFP, ENTP, ESTJ, ESFJ, ENFJ, ENTJ. The calculations must be taken with one caveat: the sample was a small convenience sample of films, and larger samples might have had different frequencies of personality types.

Still, it is interesting to note similarities and differences among the four types that are particularly overrepresented in the films. *ISFJ* was the most frequently occurring librarian type in films and is described in Briggs Myers' *Introduction to Type* as

> Quiet, friendly, responsible, and conscientious. Committed and steady in meeting their obligations. Thorough, painstaking, and accurate. Loyal, considerate, notice and remember specifics about people who are important to them, concerned with how others feel. Strive to create an orderly and harmonious environment at work and at home. (13)

An example is Marian in *The Music Man*, who says to the townspeople that the traveling salesman has given them "people to go out of your way for." *ISFP* shares an attitude (I) and two functions with ISFJ (SF), differing only in having a more flexible orientation to the outer world (P). Briggs Myers describes ISFP as "Quiet, friendly, sensitive, and kind. Enjoy the present moment, what's going on around them. Like to have their own space and to work within their own time frame. Loyal and committed to their values and to people who are important to them. Dislike disagreements and conflicts, do not force their opinions or values on others" (13). An example is prisoner-librarian Andy Dufresne in *The Shawshank Redemption*, who enjoys total involvement in music and geology and helps his fellow prisoners in a number of ways, such as providing beer, improving the prison library, and teaching one prisoner to read. *INFP* shares three letters with ISFP, and like ISFP, has Introverted Feeling as its dominant function. Briggs Myers describes this type as "Idealistic, loyal to their values and to people who are important to them. Want an external life that is congruent with their values. Curious, quick to see possibilities, can be catalysts for implementing ideas. Seek to understand people and to help them fulfill their potential. Adaptable, flexible, and accepting unless a value is threatened" (13). An example is Betty Lou Perkins in *The Gun in Betty Lou's Handbag*, who loves literature, is a creative program developer, and is most passionate when speaking at her library fundraiser. The last overrepresented type, *ESTP*, occurred in two films in which characters were portrayed as either atypical or poor librarians. In one, a librarian in a film studio archive in *Scream 3* is briefly portrayed as manipulative and unhelpful until she is bribed with a ring. In another, Mary, the main character in *Party Girl*, is portrayed in most of the film as a party-loving, outgoing, high fashion individual who contrasts in several ways with her godmother and other librarians in the film. Towards the end of the film, she appears to display more characteristics of *ISTJ*, however, the most frequent type among real librarians (Scherdin 1994). It is important to note that even though some types such as ESTP are relatively infrequent among real librarians, they are not necessarily unsuited to librarianship. Each type brings strengths and weaknesses to a profession. Briggs Myers, McCaulley, Quenk, and Hammer include an interesting table with quotes of librarians from each of the 16 personality types discussing what they like about their jobs.

If a conclusion may be drawn about the overrepresented types, it is that "positive" librarians are often portrayed as helpful and idealistic, whereas "negative" or atypical ones are often portrayed as manipulative, freewheeling, and highly extraverted. There were other kinds of negative portraits of librarians in the films: for example, the librarians in

With Honors, *Somewhere in Time*, and *The Big Sleep* are all briefly portrayed as enforcing restrictive rules and/or being unable to accept requests that are not routine. Their personality types all appeared to be ISTJ. However, the ISTJ character, Judy Lindendorf in *Party Girl* (Mary's godmother), is portrayed mostly positively, as is Bunny Watson in *Desk Set*, who has a phenomenal memory. There are several highly favorable cognitive and personal characteristics associated with the ISTJ type, such as a strong work ethic and attention to details.

The underrepresented types include many with favorable intellectual, personal, or administrative qualities found among real librarians. If the underrepresented types may be characterized as a whole, it is interesting to note that NT and ENF predominate, perhaps suggesting that filmmakers underestimate librarians' analytical/theoretical and interpersonal/persuasive/harmonizing skills.

Rank Order of Types

Comparing the rank order of personality type frequencies in the films sampled and that of real librarians allows further analysis. Table 2 displays the two rank orders side-by-side, and shows that the following types have similar ranks in the two samples: INFJ, ENFP, ENTP, ESTJ, ISTP, ESFP. The rankings for ISTJ, ESFJ, and ENFJ were less similar, but still close. The most different rankings were for ISFJ, INFP, INTJ, ISFP, ESTP, INTP, and ENTJ.

The overrepresented types have already been discussed, but this analysis shows that the most significantly underrepresented types are INTJ, INTP, and ENTJ. All of these types combine intuition with thinking, with the result that they "focus on possibilities, theoretical relationships, and abstract patterns, but they judge these from an impersonal, cause-and-effect relationship. They often pursue possibilities that are technical, scientific, theoretical, or executive where attention to the human issues may be secondary" (Briggs Myers, McCaulley, Quenk, Hammer 1998, 43).

Sex Roles

Differences of type-portraits according to gender were also investigated in this study. Nine male characters were assigned a type. Two were assigned ISFP, three were assigned ISFJ, and one each was assigned INFP, INTJ, ENTP and ENFP. These results do not appear to differ significantly from those for the female librarian characters. How-

TABLE 2. Ranks of Personality Types and Comparison with Real Librarians

Films Sample (Rank)	Scherdin	Rank
ISFJ (1)	ISTJ	(1)
ISTJ (2) INFP (3)	INTJ INTP	(2) (3)
ISFP (4)	ISFJ	(4)
ESTP, INTJ (5) (tie)	ENTJ INFP	(5) (6)
INFJ, ENFP, ENTP, ESTJ, ESFJ (6) (tie)	INFJ ESTJ ENFP ENTP ENFJ	(7) (8) (9) (10) (11)
INTP, ISTP, ENFJ, ENTJ, ESFP (7) (tie)	ESFJ ISTP ISFP ESTP ESFP	(12) (13) (14) (15) (16)

ever, the F preference is rare among males in the United States (31.4%) (Hammer and Mitchell 1996) and among males in the real librarian sample (31%) (Scherdin 1994). Portraying male librarians as preferring Feeling over Thinking and emphasizing their nurturing, gentle characteristics in some cases is used to undermine their strength or masculinity (consider, for example, Joe's hypochondriac behavior in *Joe versus the Volcano*, or Charles Halloway's initial ineffectuality in *Something Wicked This Way Comes*).

Female librarian characters are also portrayed as preferring Feeling over Thinking, which is true of 61.2% of the female population in the United States (Hammer and Miller 1996). However, in Scherdin's sample (1994), Thinking predominates among real female librarians (58%). The films in the sample appear to reinforce typical gender assumption, with females portrayed as nurturing and gentle and males in a typical "female" profession portrayed as having feminine traits.

DISCUSSION

The results reveal that filmmakers reinforce positive and negative stereotypes and sex roles in their depiction of librarians' personality types. Because personality conveys information about an individual, depicting a person's personality type will associate characteristics with him or her. With librarians, the characteristics often associated include helpfulness, idealism, or a tendency to enforce rules, as well as certain gender stereotypes. To shed further light on the issue of stereotyping of librarians, a future study might compare the personality stereotypes perpetuated in films with surveyed opinions about which personality types are typical of librarians, and which are atypical.

Conclusion

Personality type is an important tool in characterization, and as this study has shown, is an effective way to perpetuate positive and negative stereotypes and sex roles. While this study was based on a small convenience sample, it showed that films underrepresent and overrepresent some personality types compared to the distribution of types among real librarians. In addition, while the rankings of some personality type frequencies are similar between the films sample and real librarians, four types remain significantly overrepresented and three types significantly underrepresented. Films thus fail to represent the rich variety of personality characteristics found in real librarians. However, a final caveat must be added: personality type is only a partial characterization of any individual.

It is necessary to point out that such stereotyping can be a problem when associated with the Myers-Briggs system. As Kummerow discusses (2001), it is easy to stereotype minority personality types. Kummerow is an ESTJ in a mostly INFP world of the Association for Psychological Type (APT), a national organization that engages in type-related activities. She writes that she has received comments from members who say they enjoy talking with her even though she is an ESTJ. She proposes that the APT adopt more inclusive language for minority types, especially Sensing types.

The author of this article is an INTJ and writes with the biases of a person who prefers Introversion, Intuition, Thinking, and Judging. While standing by the type assignments in this paper, the author does entertain the possibility that her own personality bias may have crept in. In cases where the librarian in a film was only portrayed briefly and negatively (as being unwilling to accept deviations from the routine, or as being particularly rule enforcing), the librarian was characterized as ISTJ. While Keirsey (1998) characterizes SJs as steady, stable Guardians who preserve the status quo, the author recognizes that there was very little evidence on which to base judgment of the briefly portrayed librarians as being ISTJ. The assignments made in this paper will stand, meanwhile pointing out, that given the insidiousness and prevalence of certain stereotypes, the author may have bought into negative stereotyping about ISTJs in typing the librarian characters.

The activity of assigning types to fictional characters is not unheard-of. For example, *Bulletin of Psychological Type*, a general interest periodical published by the Association for Psychological Type, sometimes has movie reviews in which characters are typed. Thomson's *Personality Type: An Owner's Manual* also has very entertaining assignments of type to characters from popular culture, for example, from *Star Trek: The Next Generation* and other television shows.

Typing fictional characters has a certain risk, in that one faces validity questions, but it is, I believe, a good way to illustrate their creators' stereotypes about types. Buying into stereotypes about various types is an unfortunate consequence of being a consumer of popular culture, but it does make assignment of personality types to fictional characters possible.

Personality typing thus serves as a way of pointing out differences among groups of people. In other words, it can be a stereotyping tool. Filmmakers are well aware of this fact, and depict librarians as members of types with readily recognizable characteristics. This can work to the benefit or to the detriment of librarians' images, since each type has both negative and positive characteristics associated with it.

NOTE

1. People prefer one function from each of the two dichotomies.

REFERENCES

Briggs Myers, Isabel. 1990. *Gifts Differing*. 10th anniversary edition. Palo Alto, CA: Consulting Psychologists Press.

Briggs Myers, Isabel. 1998. *Introduction to Type®*. 6th edition. Palo Alto, CA: Consulting Psychologists Press.

Briggs Myers, Isabel, Mary H. McCaulley, Naomi L. Quenk, and Allen L. Hammer. 1998. *MBTI® Manual: A Guide to the Development and Use of the Myers-Briggs Type Indicator®*. 3rd edition. Palo Alto, CA: Consulting Psychologists Press, Inc.

Hammer, Allen L. and Wayne D. Mitchell. 1996. The distribution of MBTI types in the US by gender and ethnic group. *Journal of Psychological Type* 37: 2-15.

Jung, C. G. 1971. *Psychological Types*, translated by H. G. Baynes and revised by F. C. Hull. Princeton, NJ: Princeton University Press.

Keirsey, David. 1998. *Please Understand Me II: Temperament, Character, Intelligence*. Del Mar, CA: Prometheus Nemesis.

Kummerow, Jean M. 2001. "Examining Type Bias and Inclusivity: Lessons from Ethnic Identity Viewpoints." *Journal of Psychological Type*, 56, p. 6-9.

Raish, Martin. 2000. "Librarians in the Movies: An Annotated Filmography: The A Group." Available from http://www.lib.byu.edu/dept/libsci/films/agroup.html.

Scherdin, Mary Jane. 1994. Vive la différence: exploring librarian personality types using the MBTI®. p. 125-156 in *Discovering Librarians Profiles of a Profession*, edited by Mary Jane Scherdin. Chicago, IL: Association of College and Research Libraries.

Thomson, Lenore. 1998. *Personality Type: An Owner's Manual*. Boston: Shambhala.

Tieger, Paul D. and Barbara Barron-Tieger. 1998. *The Art of SpeedReading People: Harness the Power of Personality Type and Create What you Want in Business and in Life*. Canada: Little, Brown and Company.

APPENDIX

Evidence of Characters' Personality Types in Films Sample

Film	Characters and Type(s)	Selected Evidence	Extraverts Feeling
Big Sleep	Librarian (ISTJ)	Tells Bogart that he doesn't look like the type to read a book collecting book.	No
Blade	Pearl (ISFP)	Fearful, quiet.	No
Bliss	Eva (INFJ)	Discusses details of rare book. Appears decisive.	Yes
Blue Kite	Lin Shaolong (ISFJ) Li Guodong (ENFP)	Shaolong–concerned about upsetting family member. Guodong–playful.	Yes / No
Brazil	Sam Lowry (INTJ) Mr. Kurtzman (ISFJ)	Lowry–obsessed with vision of escape with girl; good with technology, systems. Kurtzman–concerned about a mistake.	No / Yes
Cal	Marcella (ISFJ)	Entertains, paints, is quiet.	Yes
The Convent	Piedade (INFP)	Interested in literature, strong ideal of purity.	No

APPENDIX (continued)

Film	Characters and Type(s)	Selected Evidence	Extraverts Feeling
Desk Set	Bunny Watson (ISTJ)	Phenomenal memory, checks budget for errors, notices Tracy's mismatching socks.	No
Foul Play	Gloria Mundy (ISFJ)	Kind to couple in the car, quiet, pleasant.	Yes
Goodbye Columbus	Neil Klugman (ENTP)	Outgoing, humorous, observant, "not a planner, a liver," critical.	Yes
The Gun in Betty Lou's Handbag	Betty Lou Perkins (INFP)	Interest in literature, has creative programming ideas, introverted.	No
Heart and Souls	Harrison Winslow (INFP)	Passion for music, dislikes aggression, appears to dislike closure.	No
Joe Versus the Volcano	Joe Banks (ISFP)	Moves in leisurely fashion, is attuned to bodily symptoms, decorates office, likes music, resourceful in times of crisis.	No
Major League	Lynn Wells (INFP)	Passion for books; graceful, artsy attire; quiet.	No
The Mummy	Evelyn "Evie" Carnahan (INTJ)	Deep knowledge of ancient documents, somewhat absent-minded (not aware of senses).	No
The Music Man	Marian (ISFJ)	Concerned with propriety, notices nature, becomes warm towards the traveling salesman, says he has caused the town to have "people to go out of your way for."	Yes
No Man of Her Own	Connie Randall (ESTJ)	Described as a handful. Assertive with Gable ("I'm very busy"). Attempts to improve Gable's organization, reminding him of appointments, etc. Gable says she "thinks of everything."	No

Film	Characters and Type(s)	Selected Evidence	Extraverts Feeling
Party Girl	Mary (ESTP) Judy Lindendorf (ISTJ)	Mary–described as major promoter, interested in parties, wardrobe. Uses Dewey Decimal System for own purposes. Judy–quiet (compared to Mary), good with details, responsible, often refers to past experiences, such as her knowledge of Mary's mother.	Yes No
Peeping Tom	Helen Stephens (ESFJ)	Friendly, offers cake to neighbor, curious, writing a children's book.	Yes
Scream 3	Librarian (ESTP)	Outgoing, knows tricks in filing system, manipulative.	Yes
The Shawshank Redemption	Andy Dufresne (ISFP)	Likes geology, music, helps friends in prison (obtains beer, develops prison library, teaches prisoner to read). Friendly but quiet.	No
A Simple Plan	Sarah Mitchell (ISFJ)	Interested in home comforts, poor intuition (develops over-complicated plans)	Yes
Sleeping with the Enemy	Sara/Laura Burney (ISFJ)	Likes to decorate, charming, quiet, good at practical plans for escaping abusive husband.	Yes
Something Wicked this Way Comes	Charles Halloway (ISFJ)	Caring, helpful, doesn't take risks	Yes
Somewhere in Time	Librarian (ISTJ)	Dislikes unroutine request to get magazines.	No
Soylent Green	Sol Roth (ISFJ)	Notices sensory details such as heat and poor food, remembers his past, loves nature.	Yes
The Spy Who Came in From the Cold	Nan Perry (ISFJ)	Likes to entertain, offers sandwich to co-worker, loyal to Communism because it "organizes our emotions."	Yes
With Honors	Librarian (ISTJ)	Tells homeless man he can't stay; rule-enforcing.	No

The Long, Strange Trip of Barbara Gordon: Images of Librarians in Comic Books

Doug Highsmith

SUMMARY. Historically, the medium of comic books and the profession of librarianship have both suffered image problems. The former is deemed unrespectable; the latter lacks the same level of prestige afforded many other professions. Does having this in common result in comic books offering images of librarians and librarianship more informed (and, therefore, more positive) than are generally to be found in other media? Or do they employ the same clichés about librarians that are the bane of so many in the profession? To examine these questions, some of the more prominent depictions of librarians in mainstream American comic books and graphic novels were reviewed . . . with mixed results. Recent depictions of librarians do seem to be more informed and more sympathetic than in the past, but even today, comic book writers still employ some of the more negative stereotypes about librarians as a way to provide their relationship with some quick and easy laughs. *[Article copies available for a fee from The Haworth Document Delivery Service: 1-800-HAWORTH. E-mail address: <docdelivery@haworthpress.com> Website: <http://www.HaworthPress.com> © 2002 by The Haworth Press, Inc. All rights reserved.]*

Doug Highsmith is Coordinator, Department of Instruction & Research Services, California State University, Hayward, CA.

The author wishes to thank Steven Bergson for providing updated information about, and additional examples of, librarians' appearances and depictions in comic book stories.

This article was based in large part on a presentation made by the author at the Popular Culture Association 29th Annual Conference in Orlando, FL in April 1998.

[Haworth co-indexing entry note]: "The Long, Strange Trip of Barbara Gordon: Images of Librarians in Comic Books." Highsmith, Doug. Co-published simultaneously in *The Reference Librarian* (The Haworth Information Press, an imprint of The Haworth Press, Inc.) No. 78, 2002, pp. 61-83; and: *The Image and Role of the Librarian* (ed: Wendi Arant, and Candace R. Benefiel) The Haworth Information Press, an imprint of The Haworth Press, Inc., 2002, pp. 61-83. Single or multiple copies of this article are available for a fee from The Haworth Document Delivery Service [1-800-HAWORTH, 9:00 a.m. - 5:00 p.m. (EST). E-mail address: docdelivery@haworthpress.com].

10.1300/J120v37n78_05

KEYWORDS. Comic books, librarians, stereotypes, social prestige, occupational status, media depiction

INTRODUCTION

Historically, the medium of comic books and the profession of librarianship have both suffered problems regarding their image with the general population. In the minds of many, comic books lack respectability. Conversely, librarians and librarianship, while certainly "respectable," are sorely lacking in prestige.

Given this shared problem with public perceptions and images, is there evidence that librarians and comic book creators view each other from an innately or instinctively sympathetic viewpoint? Do librarians naturally "relate" to comic books and similar popular culture materials in a positive manner, defending their value to skeptics in the world of academe and/or in the population at large? Conversely, do comic books offer images of librarians and librarianship more informed (and, therefore, more positive) than are generally to be found in other venues? Or do they employ the same clichés about "bookish" or "repressed" librarians that are the bane of so many members of the library profession?

Librarians' perceptions and opinions of comic books and similar popular culture materials and their place (or lack thereof) in library collections have been the focus of presentations at professional conferences and articles in the professional literature–most recently in the article "About Face: Comic Books in Library Literature," written by Allen Ellis and the present author (*Serials Review* vol. 26, no. 2 (2000)). Interested readers are referred to that article for an analysis of how librarians' opinions of comic books–as reflected in articles cited in *Library Literature*–have evolved over time.

The goal of this article is to examine the "flip side" of this issue, by looking at some of the more prominent depictions of librarians in mainstream American comic books and graphic novels. For that purpose, "mainstream American comic books and graphic novels" are defined as those published by for-profit publishers, and marketed to consumers primarily through established retail outlets such as comic book specialty shops, bookstores, and drug and grocery stores. For those unfamiliar with the term "graphic novels," these can be defined as stories told with a combination of narrative text (i.e., dialog and captions) and coordinated sequential art that appear in either a trade paperback or hardcover book format.

Among the most prominent of current for-profit publishers of comic books and graphic novels are DC Comics (a subsidiary of AOL Time Warner), Marvel Comics, Image Comics, Dark Horse Comics, and Archie Comics. Many other smaller and/or less well-known publishers are also currently active, while a variety of others were active in the industry in the past. (Prominent examples of now-defunct or inactive comic book publishers include Quality Comics, Fawcett Comics, EC Comics, Charlton Comics, First Comics, Pacific Comics, and Eclipse Comics.)

Limiting the research done for this article to comics published by major publishers was done to keep the focus on the depiction of librarians in works that were readily available to the general comic book-reading public. It was also done to exclude comic stories written by members of and/or targeted specifically to the library profession, since the purpose of the study was to gauge the images and depictions of librarians in comic book stories aimed at a mass market (or as "mass" a market as comic books command, anyway), not at the library community itself.

REVIEW OF THE LITERATURE

To confirm the assumption that the image of librarians in comic books had not been the subject of much previous research, a survey of the literature was conducted. *ERIC*, *Library Literature*, and *WorldCat* were employed for this purpose.

The search of the *ERIC* database done in March 2001 yielded no relevant records. Searching *Library Literature* using the keyword terms "Librarians and (comic books or comics)" similarly failed to locate relevant citations.

On the other hand, some sixty records were retrieved under the more general subject term of "librarians in literature" in a search of the *Library Literature* database conducted in March 2001. While not all of the documents cited in this search were examined, special mention should be made of one of the articles cited:

> "Batgirl was a librarian: Images of librarians" by Alison Hall (*Canadian Library Journal* v. 49 (Oct. '92) p. 345-7).

This article proved not to be the extensive survey of librarians in comic books that one might expect, however, given its title. In his *Librarians in Comics: Sources–Comic Books* webliography (see later section), Steven Bergson writes that this article ". . . has a good overview of our image and does (briefly) talk about Batgirl.[1] Also shows Allie [Alison Hall] in her Batgirl costume. (How many librarians dress up as other librarians on Halloween? 'Who are you supposed to be?' 'Melville Dewey, of course!' 'Who the hell's that?')."

A search of OCLC's *Worldcat* database on the topic of "Librarians AND (Comic Books or Comics)" done in March 2001 retrieved only nine (9) items. The majority of the *WorldCat* records were for books and other items that dealt with comic books in libraries or classrooms, not with the depiction of librarians in comic books.

The most relevant entries located in this search were a trio of comic books or graphic novels about librarians that had all been found in the initial 1998 search: *Adventures of the Incredible Librarian* by Joseph W. Grant (Tempe, AZ: Preservation Graphics, 1990); *The Librarian* by Penny Moran Van Horn (Scottsdale, AZ: Preservation Comics, 1988); and the 14-page *Kimberly Crochet, Librarian of Tomorrow* by Sturm and Dikkers (1988; no additional publication information available). However, none of these works were published by what would be considered for the purposes of this article to be mainstream American comics publishers, and, with the possible exception of the unviewed *Kimberly Crochet, Librarian of Tomorrow*, they appeared to be targeted primarily towards a readership of members of the library community.

Following this review of standard bibliographic tools for citations to articles relevant to this topic, more specialized resources were examined, in an effort to identify specific comic books and comic book stories that offered notable appearances by librarians as heroes, villains or supporting characters. These specialized resources included:

- The home page of the Michigan State University's Comic Arts Collection
- The previously-mentioned webliographies of Steven Bergson
- The author's private comic book collection

THE MICHIGAN STATE UNIVERSITY'S COMIC ARTS COLLECTION

The Michigan State University's Comic Arts Collection houses a significant number of comic books. Thanks to the efforts of Randall W. Scott and his colleagues, the comics in this collection have received extensive content analysis, cataloging and subject classification. Its home page <www.lib.msu.edu/comics/rri> was visited several times in preparation for this article, most recently in March 2001.

The *Reading Room Index to the Comic Art Collection* available on the site was searched using the terms "Librarians" and "Libraries." As of March 2001, only ten (10) items in the collection had been indexed under "Librarians." In addition to the three items cited from the WorldCat search, the most interesting listings[2] were for:

1. **"The Library of Souls" (Batman) / art: Jim Aparo; script: Peter Milligan; colorist: Adrienne Roy; letterer: Jim Aparo. 22 p. in Detective Comics, no. 643 (Apr. 1992).**
    SUMMARY: A murderer, who can "read people like a book," establishes the occupation of each victim and leaves the bodies in jackets with three-digit numbers on them. One victim is found in a library, and Batman notices the Dewey numbers on the books. He guesses that the killer is a librarian, though the librarian explaining the classification system to him disagrees: "That's a defamation of character. Librarians are gentle, bookish souls." But Batman is correct. (Bibliographic Information from Bill Wormstedt et al., via Grand Comic-Book Database Project.[3])

2. **"Who Is Invading Central City" (The Flash) / Don Heck, pencils; Joe Giella, inks; Cary Bates, script; Gene D'Angelo, colors; Ben Oda, letters; 12 p. in Adventure Comics, no. 465 (Sept./Oct. 1979).**
    SUMMARY: The librarian thinks the Flash (incognito) is "a strange man" because he insists that he can listen to all of the audiotapes in stock in 33 minutes. ("I'm a fast listener.") (Bibliographic Information from Martin O'Hearn, Bob Cherry and Mike Tiefenbacher of Grand Comics Database,[3] and from Steven Bergson.)

3. **"The Case of the Timid Librarian" (Chic Carter) / Vernon Henkel, story and art. 5 p. in National Comics, no. 34 (Aug. 1943).**
    NOTES: Introduction of Homer Weeks and of villain Lefty. (Bibliographic information from Lou Mougin of Grand Comic-Book Database.[3])

In addition to the ten items that were indexed under "Librarian," more than twice as many were indexed under "libraries." Of these the most relevant to this article were a pair of stories featuring Dr. Strange, in which Marvel Comics' Master of the Mystic Arts gets drawn into adventures centering on occult libraries:

1. "The Old Dark House" (Dr. Strange) / Gene Colan, pencils; Dan Green, inks; Chris Claremont, script; 17 p. in Doctor Strange, no. 39 (Feb. 1980).

   NOTES: Introduces Madeleine de St Germaine, a former love of Strange's, and Alfeo Spinosa, a priest in charge of church occult libraries, also from Strange's past. (Bibliographic information from Robert Klein of Grand Comics Database.)

2. "The Shadows of the Starstone" (Dr. Strange) / Craig Russell, pencils; Mike Esposito, Frank Giacoia, David Hunt, pencils; Gardner F. Fox, script; Mimi Gold, colors; Jean Izzo, letters; 20 p. in Marvel Premiere, no. 7 (Mar. 1973).

   SUMMARY: Henry Gordon inherits Witch House in England and discovers uncle's occult library. He finds sunken Kalumesh, and is attacked by demon Dagoth. (Bibliographic information from Gary Oppenhuis and Mike Nielsen of Grand Comics Database.)

Also listed was a story entitled "The 21st Century Film Library," which appeared in issue #48 of DC Comics' science fiction anthology title, *Strange Adventures* (September 1954). However, since the focus of this article is on the depiction and treatment of librarians as people rather than libraries as institutions or locations, and there was no indication that a librarian played any role in this story, this entry was not analyzed further.

In the course of using the *Reading Room Index*, one term for which there was a "see also" cross-reference under "Libraries" was also examined: "Captain Comet." This cross-reference exists because the superheroic Captain worked as a librarian when in his civilian identity of Adam Blake. Ten (10) entries were indexed under "Captain Comet"–indicating that Michigan State has several, but not all, of the issues of *Strange Adventures* featuring Captain Comet. Like Barbara Gordon, Adam (Captain Comet) Blake reappears later on in this article.

STEVEN BERGSON'S WEBLIOGRAPHIES

A search of the Internet on the terms "librarian(s)" and "comic books" (done using *Yahoo!*, *Google*, and *Alta Vista*), revealed one site of particular relevance to the research being done for this article: the "Libraries FAQ Homepage" <http://www.geocities.com/Athens/Acropolis/2161/>.

Available on this site were two bibliographies by Steven M. Bergson, the previously-mentioned *Librarians in Comics: Sources–Comic Books* <http://www.geocities.com/Athens/Acropolis/2161/combks/combks.htm>, and its companion, *Librarians in Comics: Sources–Comic Strips*. <http://www.geocities.com/Athens/Acropolis/2161/comstrp/comstrp.htm>.

As of March 2001 (when these sites were last visited), the bibliography on librarians in comic books listed thirty-four (34) items, most of which were comic books or graphic novels, but a few of which were other items (newspaper or magazine articles related in some way to this topic). The most recent date of any of the items included in this bibliography was February 1995.

However, in personal correspondence with the author, Mr. Bergson indicated that the webliographies are being updated, and graciously provided additional citations to relevant comic book stories (which, at the time this article was being completed, had not yet been posted on the Librarians FAQ Homepage website). In addition to the Batman and Flash stories cited above from the MSU site, the items listed in the webliography most germane to this article are listed below.

Please note that both bibliographic information and the annotations/commentary given below are by Steven M. Bergson (with some editing for space considerations by the author). Italics were added by the author of this article for emphasis. Articles are listed alphabetically by author's last name, or by title if no author is given.

1. **Baron, Mike. "Devil Fish" _Nexus_ #27 Dec. 1986.**
   A "mystic librarian" seems to transport Nexus & Judah Maccabbee to the ancient library of Alexandria. They witness its burning and try to save it.

2. **Ibid. "The Crystal Ballroom" _Nexus_ #34 July 1987.**
   A library-space station, the "Crystal Ballroom," is threatened by the Oblivoids, who want to use the library to build weapons, and then destroy the library. *When one of the citizens is asked if he lives there, he replies "Yes. We spend our lives in learning. The head librarian is chosen by lot every twenty years." The current head librarian is an elderly woman with her hair in a bun.* The Oblivoids end up being defeated through the use of sonics–i.e., noise. This predictably provokes a "This is a library! Stop! Stop!" reaction from the head librarian.

3. **Burns, Charles (writer/artist). "Doomed Marriage (?)" [3rd story]. In His Skin Deep: Tales of Doomed Romance [edited by Art Spiegelman and R. Sikoryak] (New York: Penguin, 1992).**
   The central character, not getting satisfaction at home, goes to the library to do some pleasurable reading. She befriends the li-

brarian who is courteous, helpful and friendly. She also *looks like the stereotypical librarian* (old, a woman, bifocals), but . . . later on, when the husband tries to kill the central character, the librarian saves the day, shooting him and freeing the central character who realizes she loves the librarian. There's even a lesbian kiss. Now how often are lesbian librarians represented anywhere?

4. **Batman: A Word to the Wise. (NY: DC Comics, n.d.).**

Literacy promotion Batman comic shows a branch of the Toronto Public Library and has a librarian in it. [At least they showed diversity by making her disabled. Where are the men?]

5. **Claremont, Chris (writer). "Slaughter on 10th Avenue." Marvel Team-up #83 July 1979. (NY: Marvel).**

Spider-Man can't think of where to find S.H.I.E.L.D. HQ, until he remembers how highly the city editor recommended the woman at "the morgue." (What a dreaded name for a LIBRARY!) *She is shown as unattractive (nothing new), arrogant and rude.* She does unrealistically remember the exact page number of the phone book he needs.

6. **Collins, Terry. "Situation Overdue" _Ren & Stimpy_ #35 Oct. 1995.**

Ren is interrogated by two men wearing badges (library policemen?) and *a mean-looking, stereotypical librarian (with fangs).* Ren asks Stimpy why he's coming with him to the library when he can't even read. Stimpy answers that it's Wednesday which means "lollipops, nap-time and storybook hour." The librarian with the fangs accuses Ren of being responsible for the 9-months-overdue "The Happy Squishy Bunny Book," and is taken away. Stimpy thinks Ren has been caught "abusing the photocopier" again. Ren is surprised that libraries have jail cells. He and 2 other "offenders" must stamp stacks of date due cards with the "overdue" stamp. When Ren goes berserk, he is sent back to the librarian. She is holding his burning library card and is angry with him for jumping on tables, knocking over date due cards, and, "worst of all . . . screaming in the library." He also ruined the mahogany table and a "perfectly good date due stamp." She threatens to see to it that he never gets to read another romance novel for the rest of his life. She permanently revokes his library card and tells him never to be seen at the library again "but first you must be processed." His forehead gets a permanent mark on it: DISCARD. Then the library police come in and arrest them both. Head librarian: "For burying one of our most in-demand children's books, I hereby sentence the two of you to twenty years hard labor starting with the installation of our new automated system." Ren figures it'll take decades to finish stamping computer checkout codes into every book in the library. Stimpy answers "but . . . at least the two of us will be able to sit down and enjoy some fine lit-er-ature!" And finally an open book icon with one page saying "THE END" and the other saying "Now go read a REAL book."

7. **Conway, Gerry (writer). "Reprise." Justice League of America #182 Sept. 1980 (NY: DC).**

Former felon Felix Faust tries his hand at being a librarian, only to get possessed by the spirit of an evil sorcerer whose essence had been transferred to a book in his castle. It is not explained why a seemingly ordinary library (Star City Public) has a special curator or acquires century-old books.

8. **Eisner, Will (writer/artist). "Mortal Combat." [3rd story], in Invisible People. (Princeton: Kitchen Sink Press, 1992).**

The title refers to the way that in modern urban society most of us are "invisible"–nameless, faceless, unknown–to most of the people around them. Some would say that Jews are invisible (because they are a minority) and others would say that librarians are invisible (people don't acknowledge us until they really need us . . . at five minutes to closing, yet). Eisner combines these metaphors by telling a doomed love story about 2 Jewish librarians made even more invisible by taking care of their ailing, opposite sex parent. When her father dies, she seeks romance in a male librarian (so few of these shown) who falls in love with her, but can't abandon his mother. She tries to adjust, but the jealous mother makes life difficult.

9. **Gaiman, Neil. "Season of Mists, Chapter 1" _Sandman_ (2nd series) #22 199?**

Lucien the Librarian explains to Matthew how special the library is: *"In here is every story that has ever been dreamed."*

10. **Gillis, Peter. "The Librarian" _Marvel Comics Presents_ #61 (1990) (4th story).**

Dr. Strange goes to a library, asking for the reference librarian. When Ms. Brinn (gray-haired with a bun and wearing bifocals) introduces herself, he tells her he's looking for a book on gamma-goblin immuno-history. She's about to tell him "I'm sure we have a book like that." When Stephen calls her Marjorie, she excitedly replies "Stephen?!" to which he says "Hush, Marjorie. This IS a library, you know!" (At least it wasn't HER telling HIM that). Later, Stephen tells her how he notices that she has been dyeing her hair gray. She tells Stephen that she fears that she has become immortal. Dr. Strange shows Marjorie a possible future, in which she has become an important warrior and leader: *"mankind had lost the knowledge of how to fight back. But I was there to give them back their memory!"* Marjorie says *"If I can be the memory, the living past for a distant future, then I can deal with the centuries! After all, what are librarians for?"*

11. **Golden, Christopher and Tom Sniegoski. "Beyond the Pale" _Buffy the Vampire Slayer: Giles_ #1 Oct. 2000.**

School librarian Rupert Giles returns to England to attend a funeral. While there, he realizes that a mystical menace has been unleashed and helps to defeat it. In a flashback to 1980, we see a younger Giles being warned to stay away from a certain bookshelf. "The things on that shelf are never catalogued. In fact, most council members are unaware of their existence. Nasty little trinkets best kept out of any but the most learned hands." Giles' solution is to enter "something vague" in the catalogue and "be done with it." However, when Giles is alone, he inspects certain items.

12. **Moore, John Francis (writer). "Harvest of a Quiet Eye." Doom 2099 #13 Jan. 1994 (NY: Marvel). (Reprinted in Best of Marvel 1994).**

Brother Theodore, a librarian of a small Byzantine monastery, whose job is to keep the collection hidden from outsiders, is killed by supervillain "Necrotek" while trying to access information from a database. Superpowered "Doom" performs a successful database search (cross reference visual search name and variations: nekrotek), which provides him with the spell needed to defeat Necrotek.

13. **Ostrander, John and Kim Yale. "Oracle–Year One: Born of Hope" _The Batman Chronicles_ #5 Summer 1996 (1st story).**

Barbara Gordon assumes the identity of Oracle after learning how she can use computers to fight crime and after she learns how to defend herself in her condition. A flashback panel shows her in a library, 2 patrons reading in front of a table with many books on it: "I ran one of the largest libraries on the east coast."

14. **Peterson, Scott (writer). "A Little Knowledge." Showcase 94 #12 (1st story) Dec. 1994 (NY: DC).**

Oracle (Barbara Gordon) defends herself from vengeful stalkers. Pg. 13 recounts her life story: [after her spine was shattered] "I worked with what I had." *From my days as Gotham's head librarian I knew how to find out whatever I needed. If I could do that for citizens, I could do it for colleges, non-profit corporations, private investigators and superheroes. Having been blessed with photographic recall, I studied a dozen newspapers, four dozen magazines and . . . the computer bulletin boards . . . Nowadays, I can do so much more as Oracle than I ever could do as Batgirl. There's nothing I can't find out. No problem I can't solve.*

15. **Pollack, Rachel. "Burn in the Curse" _Doom Patrol_ #64 March 1993.**

Dorothy Spinner and Dr. Magnus try to find out why her power is creating Africa-related havoc. She tells him that kids once said she was a monkey who should live in Africa. Since she wasn't allowed to go to school (they said she would scare the other children), she went to the library and got a book about Africa. Presumably, the librarians and others in the library were friendlier and/or more tolerant than those in the schools.

17. **Rosa, Don. "Guardians of the Lost Library" _Uncle $crooge Adventures_ #27 July 1994.**

Uncle Scrooge, Huey, Dewey and Louie go on a global search for the remains of the ancient library of Alexandria. Their search takes them to modern libraries and allows them to meet modern librarians. In the end they learn that the most important knowledge from the remaining books of the Alexandria library were published as the Junior Woodchuck Guidebook.

18. **Simonson, Louise. _Adventures in Reading Starring: The Amazing Spider-Man_. (New York: Marvel Comics, 1990).**

Spider-Man is fighting a villain who has a transporter ray–a fight that takes him into the Enoch Pratt Free Library. The villain fires and Spidey, as well as 3 kids that Spidey pushed into the library, are transported into different stories. In the end, Professor Eaden (not a librarian) talks about how books can be their transporters to adventure. [Author's Note: This is a special promotional "giveaway" comic, and not part of the regular Spider-Man series. It has been included here despite the absence of an actual librarian in it.]

19. **Suess, Jeff. "The Lit-Wit Issue" _Animaniacs_ #49 June 1999.**

   The Animaniacs are in a library: "This, sibs, is what movies are before they're born." "Wow, lookit all the square things with paper!" *The stereotypical, bunned, elderly, grim-looking woman librarian shushes them. "So, where are the books with pictures?" "Comic books? No No No! We only have high literature here . . . Literature does not have silly cartoons. That's so juvenile."* Final page: Smiling librarian: "Oh yes! Comics are incredible! I never realized how expressive they could be!" Her next word balloon is written over by the word balloons of 2 of the Warners, but we can make out certain words and phrases: "remarkable how the . . . and pictures play off . . . be telling as . . . prose. My word, imagine the art if Hemingway . . . I've completely . . . my opinion . . . "

Mr. Bergson's bibliography on librarians in comic strips is approximately three times as large as the one on comic books. Many of the citations offer interesting descriptions of depictions of librarians in various comic strips or one-panel cartoons. While an analysis of the image of librarians in comic strips and cartoons, as opposed to comic books and graphic novels, falls outside of the scope of this article, Mr. Bergson's webliography is well worth reviewing by anyone interested in this subject.

PRIVATE COMIC BOOK COLLECTION

The MSU database and the webliographies of Steven Bergson allow the interested researcher to identify several specific comic book stories in which librarians play a notable role. They demonstrate that the classic cliché of the librarian as an older woman whose hair is in a bun and who loves nothing better than to "shush" overly boisterous library patrons, is far from unknown in comic books of recent vintage–both in traditional super-hero fare such stories starring Batman, Dr. Strange and their colorful colleagues, and in humorous titles such as *Ren & Stimpy* and *Animaniacs.*

Using these resources, the researcher is also able to find citations to stories that clearly reflect favorably upon libraries as institutions, and librarians as professionals dedicated to the preservation of knowledge. And, thanks to these bibliographic tools, the researcher is made aware–to some extent, at least–of the presence in comic books of specific characters germane to the topic (e.g., Batgirl/Oracle, Captain Comet, Rupert Giles, and Lucien the Librarian).

However, it cannot be said that simply by using these resources one would come away with a clear understanding of the rather convoluted career of Barbara Gordon, a.k.a. Batgirl, a.k.a. Oracle, or with a full appreciation of the role and personality of Lucien the Librarian. As valuable as they are, neither of Mr. Bergson's bibliographies nor the information available from MSU can be considered exhaustive or definitive compilations on the topic of the depiction of librarians in comic books.

Indeed, as anyone who has ever done research in comic books is aware, indexes that identify or classify specific comic book stories by theme or subject are few, far between, and far from comprehensive. While this situation is certainly improving, thanks to the efforts of people like Stephen Bergson, MSU's Randall Scott and the compilers of the Grand Comic-Book Database, there is still quite a long way to go.

Even at the start of the twenty-first century, researchers in this area often find themselves having to rely largely on personal knowledge and private collections. In the present instance, the author had access to a personal collection that at its largest numbered approximately 35,000 comic books–albeit an access limited by the current location and sheer size of that collection.

Still, access (however limited) to a personal collection did help the author recall to mind the character of Vera, the quiet-but-attractive bespectacled librarian girl friend of Hank (Beast) McCoy in the pages of the *X-Men* comic book of the 1960s. More importantly, it made possible a fuller examination of the careers of some of the most significant examples of the depiction of librarians in American mainstream comic books.

The remainder of this article will focus on five characters, who between them arguably offer the most significant examples of the use of librarians as major characters in mainstream comics. These characters are: Adam (Captain Comet) Blake; Lucien the Librarian, from the pages of Neil Gaiman's *The Sandman*; *Buffy the Vampire Slayer*'s Rubert Giles; Barbara (Batgirl/Oracle) Gordon; and, finally, Superman's Kryptonian mother, Lara.

CAPTAIN COMET

In a number of respects, Captain Comet was a character ahead of his time. A costumed super-hero, his debut in *Strange Adventure* 9 (June 1951) occurred about 5 years before the so-called Silver Age of super-hero comics was ushered in by the appearance of the second version of the Flash in *Showcase 4* (Sept.-Oct. 1956). By the time super-heroes were popular once again, Captain Comet's career had already drawn to a close, ending in *Strange Adventures* 49 (October 1954)–although the character was revived in the 1970s and has been a sporadic presence in DC Comics publications ever since.

Captain Comet was also very much ahead of his time in the way he got his powers: he was mutant. As even the most casual comics fan is probably aware, Marvel Comics' *X-Men* books have captured a significant share of the super-hero marketplace for nearly two decades now. The X-Men and the members of their myriad spin-off companion teams are . . . mutants! And the original X-men didn't even show up until 1963–a good dozen years after Captain Comet had blazed a trail for them.

Finally, Captain Comet was most literally a man ahead of his time in that his mutant powers were that he had the abilities of a human being from 100,000 years in the future. This meant that he had not only a variety of physical skills and attributes sorely lacking in mundane homo sapiens, but, most importantly, he had a super-mind so advanced that it wouldn't be standard issue for the bulk of humanity for another 100,000 years. How did he put these great mental powers to work? As it happens, when he wasn't wearing a reddish spaceman's costume to fight crime or stave off alien invasions, he was working in a library. More specifically, he was a reference librarian in an academic library. What better use for a super-mind? And what better way to show that at least some comics writers found librarianship a noble occupation for a heroic character?

On balance, Captain Comet certainly offers a very positive image for librarians in comics, but this conclusion comes with a couple of caveats. Captain Comet–or, more accurately, Adam Blake, his true identity–was referred to as an "information clerk" rather than a reference librarian. Although there is no definitive way to gauge his educational background, there seems to be no hard evidence to show that Mr. Blake went to library school. Perhaps more importantly in the context of this article, there was no evidence in any of the Captain Comet stories read by the author to indicate that his writers were aware that this would have been the appropriate career path for someone with his position in a library to have taken.

Those few times Adam Blake is actually shown working at his day job, he's embodying another cliché (albeit an arguably more positive one than the repressed, spinster female librarian): the "answer man" who can provide the correct response to any query without resorting to doing any research. Ask him a question and he'll rattle off the answer without leaving his seat or consulting a reference source of any kind. But then again, he does have a super-mind.

LUCIEN THE LIBRARIAN

Captain Comet epitomizes the science fiction-based superhero popular in the 1950s and 1960s at DC and other comics publishers. It's difficult to think of characters who stand in starker contrast to this type than those who inhabit the rich fantasy world of one of the premiere comic book writers of his day (or any other, for that matter)–Neil Gaiman. Gaiman's magnum opus is, of course, *Sandman*–a 75-issue masterpiece which stands as not only the greatest achievement in the fantasy genre the comics medium has ever seen, but as arguably the greatest regularly-published comic book of all time.

The Sandman (Morpheus) is an immortal (or more accurately, "Endless") being who presides over the Dreaming, a realm populated by numerous colorful characters. One of the most fascinating of the Sandman's supporting cast is Lucien the Librarian.

Lucien is in charge of what is literally the "dream" library, in that it houses not only the greatest books ever written, but also the greatest books *never* written. In this library can be found not only a complete set of Shakespeare portfolios, but also works of the Bard that exist nowhere else. In many respects, Lucien can lay claim to being comics' "ultimate" librarian, and a very sympathetically drawn one, at that. Fussy, obsessive and occasionally supercilious, he is nonetheless a concerned and caring individual–for all that he is not even "real."

As with Captain Comet, Lucien offers what is on balance a positive image of librarians in comic books. The main caveat one might raise with Lucien is that he represents, if not exactly a type of amateur librarian, than at least a "pre-professional" one. He is basically a scholarly being given a sinecure in the library, who does not appear to have received any specialized training for this undertaking. He maintains the collection of and for his lord and master, Morpheus. Although other denizens of the Dreaming are allowed access to Lucien's library, he is really serving a clientele of one.

While there is certainly nothing wrong with this–especially in the context of *Sandman*–Lucien doesn't really contribute much to the image of the librarian as a specially educated information professional. On the other hand, he is the epitome of the image of librarian as bibliophile.

RUPERT GILES

Of all the characters being discussed for this article, only one has (thus far, at least) achieved a professional accolade afforded to but a few librarians–appearing on the cover of an issue of *American Libraries*. That character is, of course, Rubert Giles, erstwhile school librarian of Sunnyvale, CA High School, and mentor and friend of Sunnyvale's most famous alumna, Buffy the Vampire Slayer.

Buffy made her debut as the eponymous star of a big screen movie, and moved on to even greater fame as the protagonist of a highly rated weekly television series. The popularity of the television version of Buffy served as a springboard for her 1998 move into comic books, courtesy of comic book publisher Dark Horse.

Naturally enough, when Buffy moved into the comic book medium, so too did her colorful cast of supporting characters, including Rupert Giles (who, like most of Buffy's supporting cast, had made his debut in the TV series rather than on the silver screen). As was the case with other members of the co-called "Scooby Gang," Rubert was even tapped to star in his one one-shot comic book special, *Buffy the Vampire Slayer: Giles* (October 2000; cited above), as well as solo short stories such as "Hello Moon" from *Dark Horse Comics Presents* 141 (March 1999).

So, Rupert Giles has had a comic book career, which, while fairly brief, is both notable and ongoing. However, it must be noted that Rupert, unlike the other characters being discussed herein, is not original to the comic book medium. Thus his depiction in comic books is less a reflection of the treatment of librarians in that medium than it is an adherence to Joss Whedon's original source materials by those given the task of adapting Buffy's adventures into the comic book format.

Moreover, while Rupert's careers as Watcher and comic book character are indeed ongoing, his career as a librarian may well be over. As was the case with his television counterpart, the comic book version of Rubert Giles has given up his position as librarian at Sunnyvale High to open an occult book store near the University of California, Sunnyvale campus, so as to be in a better position to continue his role as mentor and confidant to college student Buffy Summers. While this deprives the library profession of a high profile positive role model, it must in fairness be noted that this was a change dictated by Buffy's graduation from high school. Besides, Rupert Giles is hardly the first librarian to effect a mid-life career change by opening a bookstore.

BATGIRL

A big screen version of Batgirl joined the "Batman" movie series as a major character in 1997's much vilified *Batman and Robin*. Portrayed by popular young actress Alicia Silverstone, the movie version of Batgirl was in "real" life the 15-year-old niece of Bruce Wayne's butler, Alfred (Penneyworth). Meanwhile (as they say in comics), 1999 saw the appearance of a completely different character with no familial relationship to Alfred (or any other member of the Batman "family" of characters) also sporting the name of "Batgirl." Originally popping up in the pages of various Batman-related comic books from DC Comics, this version of Batgirl has proven to be so popular that she has been awarded her own on-going monthly comic book title.

However, as longtime fans of the *Batman* comics and/or of the faddishly popular 1960s "Batman" TV series are well aware, the best-known version of Batgirl was "really" Barbara Gordon, the twenty- (or thirty-) something daughter of Gotham City's much put-upon Police Commissioner, James Gordon. Barbara/Batgirl made her debut in the pages of *Detective Comics* 359 (January 1967) in the Batman story entitled "The Million Dollar Debut of Batgirl," by Carmine Infantino (penciller), Sid Greene (inker), and Julius Schwartz (editor).

In the course of her "million dollar debut," readers discover that when she is not fighting crime as Batgirl, Barbara Gordon is the recently hired head of the Gotham City Public Library. Moreover, Barbara is no humble possessor of an MLS degree–she is *Dr*. Barbara Gordon, proud possessor of a Ph.D. in library science.

This is certainly heady stuff as regards the depiction of librarians in comic books. After all, this was the height of the Batman television show craze, and the Caped Crusader was undeniably the era's single most popular comic book character. And why was Batgirl showing up at just this time? Why, so that her debut in the comics would coincide with her appearance as a new regular character in the television show's second season!

Clearly Batgirl was one of the highest profile characters to come on the scene at what was the apex of the resurgence of comics' popularity during the industry's so-called "Silver Age." And, of all the civilian identities she could have been given, the powers-that-be at DC Comics opted to make her a library professional. As a cliché-inclined writer might exclaim, "Holy Dewey Decimal, Batman!"

Does this version of Batgirl, especially when taken in conjunction with the other characters already discussed, offer proof positive that librarianship was a valued and honored profession in the pages of mainstream American comic books–even at a time when comics were far from respectable in the eyes of many in the library profession? Surely the occupation chosen for Batgirl's civilian identity offers compelling evidence of the high regard comic book creators had (and have) for librarians, their fellow sufferers-in-the-court-of-public-opinion. Why else make one of their biggest new stars of the era a member of this august profession?

Nor is Barbara Gordon just any librarian. She is the head of what is presumably one of the largest public libraries in the DC Comics version of reality (since Gotham City is more or less a stand-in for New York City).

But how is she shown going about her duties when we first meet her in her civilian identity? How is the chief administrator of a library that clearly must have a multi-million-volume collection, a multi-million-dollar budget, and a staff that probably numbers in the hundreds, shown spending her time? She is shown reshelving books and working at the Circulation Counter–both worthy and necessary activities in a library of any size, but not likely to rank high on a head librarian's personal "to do" list.

And what is her physical appearance? She's shown wearing glasses (which, since she's also the ultra-athletic Batgirl, she doesn't really need). Her hair is tied up tightly in a bun. And she's wearing traditional conservative–not to say dowdy–clothing. In other words, she embodies the stereotypical image of the female librarian of the day–busy doing clerical tasks while attired and made up in such a way as to guarantee to minimize whatever physical attractiveness she might possess beneath her frumpy exterior.

Admittedly, like all the rest of DC's super-heroes active during the mid-1960s, Batgirl was obsessed with keeping her true identity a secret. In her case, she feared not only being found out by her enemies, but by her father, the police commissioner, and her allies, Batman and Robin–all of whom would presumably insist that she abandon her costumed identity should they learn the truth. So in the context of the stories, it's not only understandable that Barbara Gordon would act and dress in a manner guaranteed to minimize suspicion that she is in fact the crime fighting Batgirl, it is to be expected. Even taking this into account, though, it is difficult to believe that making Batgirl a librarian in her other identity is a sign of any particular sympathy for librarians and their image in the popular media on the part of the editors and writers at DC Comics.

More likely explanations for why Batgirl's alter ego was a librarian are (a) librarianship was at the time an established and acceptable occupation for a(n) (unmarried) young woman, and (b) Barbara Gordon's job as a seemingly meek and passive librarian had to be considered an ideal contrast to her truly significant (and exciting) work as Batgirl. There may be a story or two from this era wherein Barbara Gordon is shown using her information-locating skills in the pursuit of bad guys (a seemingly logical plot device given that Batgirl's role model, the Batman, laid claim to the title of World's Greatest Detective), but no such examples were located while research for this article was being done.

Indeed, Barbara Gordon's career as a librarian meant so little to the writers (and, presumably, to her), that she eventually abandoned it. This change was made some time after the character had graduated from being an occasional co-star in the pages of the "Batman" series to starring in her own solo series in the pages of *Detective Comics* (albeit in a second-stringer position to Batman's adventures). In the 1970s, with the bloom long off the "Batman" TV craze and sales of comic books on the wane, the writers were clearly casting about for ways to make the character more compelling and the series more interesting. And to be fair, they gave her a career switch that even most librarians would consider a step up. They made her a member of Congress. Major Owens was not the first!

To put the best face on it, this career change could be seen as reflecting the increased opportunities women were seen as having after the advent of Women's Liberation. On the other hand, it could just as legitimately be seen as an admission by the strip's writers that being a "mere" librarian was too dull and uninteresting a job with which to saddle a character doing her best to hang on to a monthly slot in one of DC Comics' flagship titles.

Although it doubtless seemed a good idea at the time, the change of career and the change of locale (Washington, D.C., rather than Gotham

City) did little to rekindle interest in this series. Nor did Barbara Gordon distinguish herself in any particular way as a member of the House. The exact circumstances surrounding the end of Barbara Gordon's congressional career have been lost in the mists of time, but nothing could be located in the *Congressional Record* or elsewhere that would indicate that this career was a particularly distinguished one. But while Barbara Gordon's congressional career may have ended with a whimper, her Batgirl career certainly came to an end with a bang–literally.

This occurred long after her own series wound down, and her appearances were now limited primarily to popping up in the occasional Batman story. One such story was *Batman: The Killing Joke*, a special event, ultra-deluxe comic book published in 1988. Written by one of the best writers in the business, Alan Moore, and penciled and inked by talented artist Brian Bolland, the story depicts Batgirl as being outmaneuvered and trapped by Batman's deadliest foe, the Joker. The crazed clown then proceeds to shoot his captive at point blank range. Although her life is saved, Barbara Gordon is left a paraplegic, her Batgirl career clearly a thing of the past.

ORACLE

However, instead of fading off into comic book character limbo, Barbara Gordon re-invented herself, re-discovered the information finding talents that her library science background had provided her, and re-emerged as a credible, if initially improbable crime fighter under the codename of Oracle. As Oracle, Barbara Gordon is arguably the first true librarian-as-super-hero yet seen in a mainstream comic book (as opposed to super-hero who happens to be a librarian in his/her private life).

Operating primarily from her apartment, Oracle puts to full use the information science skills Barbara Gordon learned on her way to her Ph.D. Teamed with the dynamic Black Canary, Oracle forms one half of the "Birds of Prey," stars of their own monthly comic book. Not only that, but Oracle doubles as an occasional member of DC Comics' premiere super-team, the Justice League of America.

Putting her information gathering and analysis skills to use in thwarting the schemes of both costumed super-baddies as well as more mundane gangsters and white-collar criminals, the physically challenged but superbly resourceful Oracle occupies a unique place in the annals of superhero-dom the "information goddess" as crime stopper.

Already noted in the excerpts from Steven Bergson's bibliography provided above, Barbara Gordon's own musing on her new modus operandi as shown in the pages of *Showcase '94* #12 (December 1994) bears repeating: "From my days as Gotham's head librarian I knew how to find out whatever I needed. . . . Nowadays I can do so much more as Oracle than I ever could do as Batgirl. There's nothing I can't find out. No problem I can't solve."

The writer of that particular story was Scott Peterson, while the other Oracle story cited above was written by John Ostrander and Kim Yale. However, the writer most responsible for the "rebirth" of Barbara Gordon in the guise of Oracle has been Barbara Kesel. Ms. Kesel's affinity for the character is understandable, as she is one of the few writers (indeed, perhaps the only one) currently working in the mainstream comic book medium who possesses a degree in library and information sciences. Thus it is not terribly surprising to find that Oracle offers an extremely positive depiction of a librarian in the comic book medium.

SUPERMAN'S MOM, LARA THE LIBRARIAN

Most long-lived comic book super-heroes have seen changes made to their origins and histories, modified over the years by some of the many writers who have handled their adventures. These modifications have varied from rather minor revisions and additions, to complete "reboots" wherein whole chunks of the career and personal and familial biography of the hero are effectively declared null and void–thus freeing the writer to make wholesale changes and "improvements" in the character without being constrained by his (or her) established history.

When he took over the Superman franchise in 1986, writer/artist John Byrne made a variety of changes and modifications in the lore and legend of the Man of Steel. One such change was to give baby Kal-El's mother, Lara–who heretofore had been depicted by and large as a Kryptonian version of a traditional housewife–a profession and a career to call her own. The career he selected for her: librarianship!

While subsequent modifications in Superman's history and "back story" call into question whether this version of Lara's career is still the "official" one endorsed by DC Comics' publishers and Superman's current editors and writers, it is still well worth noting. And who better to sum things up than the Man of Steel himself? In the pages of *World of Krypton* #4 (March 1988), Superman tells his future wife, Lois Lane, some of the facts he knows about his parents on doomed Krypton.

He says, "My mother, Lois, [was a] young librarian named Lara. You should know that on Krypton the job of librarian was one of the most highly esteemed. Lara's task was the care and maintenance of the central data banks. The vast repository of Kryptonian history and science."

Needless to say, planet Krypton had a highly advanced civilization–one centuries ahead of any on Earth. Clearly the peoples of Earth could learn much from it about the value of those who enter the noble profession of librarianship–even if Krypton did blow up.

CONCLUSION

Oracle, Captain Comet, Lucien the Librarian, Rupert Giles and (John Byrne's version of) Superman's Kryptonian birth mother, Lara, all offer positive depictions of librarians in mainstream American comic books. However, with exploration of this topic far from complete, it is at the very least premature to state that comic book writers and editors are uniquely or even unusually sensitive in their treatment of librarians in their stories–or that they possess any innate or instinctive sympathy with librarians as members of a profession which, like their own, has its image problems with the general public. Even in the twenty-first century, an intelligent and accomplished writer like Peter David can indulge in a sight gag in the pages of DC Comics' *Young Justice* 31 (April 2001) wherein the young super-speedster Impulse is the recipient of a collective "Shhh . . . !" when he has the poor judgment to disrupt the otherwise silent "Librarians Book Faire." Nor is this a unique example of librarian clichés and stereotypes being employed in the pages of mainstream comic books.

Like other mass media, comic books often find it easiest to amuse or entertain their audience by going for the quick payoff afforded by communicating via the "shorthand" of commonly held and easily recognizable archetypes and stereotypes. The introverted, mousy, shush-ing librarian is undeniably one such stereotype that continues to pop up in comic books. So long as such stereotypical images exist in the population as a whole, they will continue to be employed from time to time in a medium of popular entertainment such as comic books.

Happily, such depictions have been counterbalanced by more positive treatments of librarians in comic book stories of various genres. If it cannot be said that comic book writers are especially sensitized to the image problems experienced by the library profession, neither can it be compellingly argued that librarians are a particular victim of misunderstanding and mistreatment at the hands of comic book writers.

NOTES

1. The career of Barbara (Batgirl) Gordon will be chronicled in considerable detail later in this article.

2. Bibliographic information and story summaries taken from the *Reading Room Index to the Comic Art Collection*. They have been edited by the author for space considerations.

3. The Grand Comic-Book Database Project <www.comics.org> is an on-going effort to build a database which will contain information on creator credits, story details, and other information useful to the comic book reader and fan "for every comic book ever published." Unfortunately, the Database is not currently searchable under subject terms such as "librarian(s)." A review by David S. Serchay of the Grand Comic-Book Database Project appeared in the October 1, 1999 issue of *Library Journal* (page 32).

Librarians in Children's Literature, 1909-2000

Elaine Yontz

SUMMARY. The presentations of librarians in thirty-five children's books published between 1909 and 2000 in the United States were described, compared, and analyzed to discover indications of attitudes and beliefs about librarians and to discern evidence of changing roles within the profession of librarianship. In regard to gender and ethnicity, most of the librarians depicted are female and Caucasian, including those in books from recent decades.

Consistency in work tasks of librarians is seen throughout the century, but the tools used to perform the work show consistent evolution. Librarians emerge as caring, friendly, and energetic professionals who have positive interactions and relationships with patrons. *[Article copies available for a fee from The Haworth Document Delivery Service: 1-800-HAWORTH. E-mail address: <docdelivery@haworthpress.com> Website: <http://www. HaworthPress.com> © 2002 by The Haworth Press, Inc. All rights reserved.]*

KEYWORDS. Librarians, librarianship, history, children's literature, roles

Elaine Yontz is Associate Professor, Valdosta State University, 1500 North Patterson Street, Valdosta, GA 31698-0150 (E-mail: eyontz@valdosta.edu).

The author gratefully acknowledges the valuable research assistance contributions of: Elizabeth D. Engel, University of South Florida SLIS; Rita Smith, Baldwin Library of Historical Children's Literature; and Jack Randall Fisher II, George Smathers Libraries.

[Haworth co-indexing entry note]: "Librarians in Children's Literature, 1909-2000." Yontz, Elaine. Co-published simultaneously in *The Reference Librarian* (The Haworth Information Press, an imprint of The Haworth Press, Inc.) No. 78, 2002, pp. 85-96; and: *The Image and Role of the Librarian* (ed: Wendi Arant, and Candace R. Benefiel) The Haworth Information Press, an imprint of The Haworth Press, Inc., 2002, pp. 85-96. Single or multiple copies of this article are available for a fee from The Haworth Document Delivery Service [1-800-HAWORTH, 9:00 a.m. - 5:00 p.m. (EST). E-mail address: docdelivery@haworthpress.com].

10.1300/J120v37n78_06

Literature written for children offers a valuable window into the attitudes and values of the surrounding culture. Because adults strive to instill their most respected beliefs and values into their children, the writers and publishers of juvenile materials reveal themselves through their choices of content. As R. Gordon Kelly has written, ". . . children's literature is significant and illuminating for the cultural historian because it constitutes one important way in which the adult community deliberately and self-consciously seeks to explain, interpret, and justify that body of beliefs, values, attitudes, and practices which, taken together, define in large measure a culture. . . ."[1]

The goals of this study are to describe, compare, and analyze the presentations of librarians in selected children's books published throughout the twentieth century in the United States. The texts and illustrations in thirty-five fiction and non-fiction books published between 1909 and 2000 have been examined. Areas of focus have included the gender and ethnicity of the librarians, descriptions of the librarians' work tasks, the tools used by librarians, and the nature and quality of interactions between librarians and patrons. The purposes of the research are to uncover indications of attitudes and beliefs about librarians and to discern evidence of changing roles within the profession of librarianship.

Children's literature has been underutilized as source material for historical research in many disciplines, including librarianship. These primary sources offer a unique, relatively unexplored vantage point from which to view changes in the image and role of the librarian.

LITERATURE REVIEW

An analysis of the existing literature indicates that the use of historical children's literature to study the cultural history of librarianship is in its infancy.

The authors of previous studies of librarians in children's literature have been interested in the image of the librarians portrayed and in the possible effects on children's attitudes toward libraries and librarians. Norman Stevens has described books published from 1937 to the present.[2] He has concluded that recent years have seen a notable increase in the number of children's books which include librarians and libraries and that the portrayal of librarians in such publications is more positive than was true in the past. He encourages the use of current books to engender positive attitudes toward libraries and librarians.[3] Katherine M. Heylman studied 22 books for children published between 1932 and

1975. She found that typically the librarians depicted are female and have positive attitudes toward patrons.[4] Jill E. Buie's 1997 examination of 18 children's books published after 1975 reached conclusions similar to Heylman's.[5]

Three master's theses have focused on particular types of books. Mary Ellen Davis examined twenty picture books aimed at children in the primary grades, for the purpose of determining whether the books presented positive role models or stereotypical views of librarians. She found that most of the librarians portrayed were young, pleasant women and that very few male or minority librarians were included.[6] Ruby Othella Denman and Virginia McNiel Speiden each examined a small number of career-related books. Denman, who studied seven "teenage career books" published near the time of her writing in the 1950s, concluded that librarianship was presented accurately and in a positive light.[7] Speiden's thesis, which was unavailable for review for the present study, describes eight "library career novels."[8]

There is room for more research in this area. A larger number of more extensive studies should be done. Continued investigation along this path should expand our knowledge and offer new avenues for further research.

DESIGN AND PROCEDURES OF THE STUDY

The present study differs from previous efforts by seeking evidence of the changing of librarians' roles over time. The current project includes publications from a wider expanse of time and includes a slightly larger number of books than did previous studies.

Thirty-five fiction and nonfiction books for children published between 1909 and 2000 were chosen for examination. Items selected were accessible to the researcher within the time limitations of the study. Strong efforts were made to locate examples published in each decade of the twentieth century. Most titles were chosen from the Baldwin Library of Historical Children's Literature at the University of Florida. Other items were located in the circulating collections of the University of Florida and the University of South Florida Libraries and in the Bronson Public Library of the Levy County, Florida, Public Library System. Within these libraries, some titles were discovered through the use of LCSH and ACC subject-heading searches in the online catalogs. Keyword searching using variations of "librarian" and "library" revealed some partially-cataloged titles. Printed issues of the *Children's Catalog*,[9] which include subject analysis at the chapter level, were used to identify additional titles. Shelf browsing in the 020 range was also utilized. Where possible, five books from each decade were included. In other cases, as many titles as were accessible from each decade were used.

The text and illustrations in each book were examined. Notes were taken on the gender and ethnicity of the librarians depicted, descriptions of the librarians' work tasks, the tools used by librarians, and the nature and quality of interactions between librarians and patrons. A system of abbreviations for work tasks and tools was developed to aid in coding and analysis. The data collected were input into a database program using Microsoft Works software, so that comparisons could be made and trends observed. The Microsoft Works database provided a combination of ease of use and data manipulation capacities, which were adequate for the project.

FINDINGS OF THE STUDY

Gender/Ethnicity

The librarians depicted are predominantly white females. This is true for the sample as a whole and for the books published in more recent decades. The percentage changes in the direction of greater diversity after 1970.

There were 194 portrayals of librarians identified. Of this total, 71.6% were white females, 17% were white males, 7.7% were African-American females, 2.6% were African-American males, .5% were Hispanic males, and .5% were Asian-American females. Of the white males depicted, 21.2% were historical figures; in all but one of these instances, the historical figure was Melvil Dewey. Overall, 88.6% of the librarians identified in the study were Caucasian.

In the decades before 1970, no depictions of librarians of color were seen. In the decades beginning with the 1970s, change was noted in the direction of greater diversity. After 1970, 61.4% of the librarians identified were white females, 16.8% were white males, 14.9% were African-American females, 5% were African-American males, 1% were Hispanic males, and 1% were Asian-American females.

Work Tasks and Tools

Librarians' work tasks, as depicted in these books, have maintained consistency over the decades of the twentieth century. Most of the tasks identified are repeated in numerous books and in each decade represented in the study. Reference, readers' advisory, story hours for children, circulation, selection, acquisition, cataloging, processing, public relations, outreach, administration, mounting of exhibits, and programming are areas of work which were seen in every decade examined and which are familiar to working librarians of today. Even the mundane activities of dusting and arranging chairs and the unevenly-appreciated task of attending meetings appear in literary librarians' lives in each decade studied.

A few tasks are seen sporadically. Bibliographic instruction, defined here as planned instruction in library use to a group of patrons larger than three, appears in the 1940s[10] and 1950s,[11] then disappears. Interlibrary loan appears during the 1960s[12] and 1970s.[13] Professional travel rated a mention during the 1920s,[14] and writing for publication was mentioned twice, once during the 1920s[15] and again during the 1930s.[16]

In contrast to the relative stability of librarians' work tasks, the tools used to accomplish these tasks show change over the decades. Books are shown as important library tools in all decades and in every individual item studied. Magazines are included in the 1909 library,[17] and magazines and newspapers are mentioned as library tools consistently starting in the decade of the 1930s. Audiovisual materials first appear as library materials in 1959.[18] Nonprint materials are part of libraries in 14 of the 21 books published after 1959.

The card catalog is the most commonly mentioned catalog, appearing in fifteen of the thirty-five books, including in items with publication dates as late as 1993[19] and 2000.[20] Alternative forms of catalogs begin to be mentioned in the late 1970s, when Hardendorff broaches the possibility of a microform catalog.[21] Computer catalogs appear in three of the five books examined from the 1980s.[22] The Internet is mentioned in 1996[23] and 2000.[24]

Striking changes in the tools used in circulation can be seen. Books from the earlier decades repeatedly mention cards, many of them colored, and stamps. A "dating pencil," for writing patron information on a card then stamping the due date, is mentioned in 1938[25] and again in 1957.[26] A "charging machine" appears in 1977.[27] A security gate can be seen in Deedy's 1994 picture book.[28]

A major tool for outreach is the bookmobile. The bookmobile plays a major role in Lingenfelter's novel of 1938[29] and in de Leeuw's of 1945.[30] The bookmobile appears as one of several library tools in occasional publications during the 1950s,[31] 1960s,[32] 1970s,[33] and 1990s.[34]

The first appearance of an assistive technology for patrons with special needs is seen in de Leeuw's 1945 novel,[35] when enterprising Anne procures the new talking books on phonodisc for a blind shut-in. Assistive technologies are again mentioned in two publications in the 1990s by McClymont[36] and Munro.[37]

Interactions Between Librarians and Patrons

Librarians as depicted in this group of books are helpful, caring, service-oriented members of the community who have supportive encounters and positive relationships with library patrons. The protagonist in Pfaender's 1954 novel exemplifies the predominant librarian's stance when she asserts, ". . . the richest treasure a librarian knows is sharing the lives of the people who come to her library."[38] The starkly negative icon of terror is noticeably absent from this group of books.

In thirty of the thirty-five books, the librarians are portrayed as unequivocally positive characters. In one book,[39] the librarian begins the story as a "dragon" but is converted into a child-centered object of affection by the end of the story. In four books, librarians are either minimally depicted or absent.

A change in the librarians' role as readers' advisors over the decades is evident. Through 1945, the librarian's job includes the promotion of "good" books to patrons. Such materials as novels and travel books are acceptable in libraries, but only as lures. This approach is clearly indicated in the following exchange between Dorcas and Polly, as they discuss the gift books they expect to receive for their fledgling town library:

> "Such a lot of trash as we'll get!" groaned Dorcas.
>
> "I know it," assented Polly, "but they will all take an interest, and that is what we are after now. Once properly established, we can buy good books, and these old ones will just stand idle or wear out or get lost or something."[40]

After 1945, the emphasis on differentiating between better and worse reading material disappears, and librarians help patrons to find what they want. The newer attitude is typified by McClymont's assurance that librarians " . . . will help you find the kind of book you enjoy."[41]

Four books, published between 1964 and 1988, can be described as deemphasizing librarians. In these works, mention of librarians is either minimal or totally lacking. The library is seen as a collection of materials, and patrons are depicted as finding their own materials. Shor exemplifies this attitude in 1964 by writing, "Libraries everywhere will always be your friends."[42]

DISCUSSION

Among the librarians portrayed in this group of books, the predominance of white females in all decades is striking. Though the depictions of librarians do change in the direction of greater diversity after 1970, the drop of white females from 71.6% to 61.4% is less than might have been expected or hoped. This change indicates some broader perception of librarianship as a field in which a wide variety of people can participate. Any change in the direction of greater inclusiveness is to be applauded. Nevertheless, it is obvious that efforts to diversify the profession need to continue and to be vigorously pursued.

The findings of this study are in concert with previous studies in revealing a preponderance of positive descriptions of librarians. This result is in interesting contrast to librarians' often-expressed concern that the public may view them in a negative light.[43] Heylman suggests that these positive portrayals may be the result of attempts to sell books to librarians or may stem from the fact that people who become authors may have more positive experiences with librarians than is the norm. She also points out that some of the authors are librarians themselves.[44] Heylman's explanations certainly have merit. Surely, though, it is possible that these positive images are evidence of sincere appreciation for librarians and their contributions on the part of at least some members of the public.

These books show librarians as "early adapters" of new technologies over several decades. The tasks performed by librarians showed noticeable consistency, but the tools used to carry out the tasks evolved continuously. Charging machines, bookmobiles, books on phonodisc, microform readers, computer catalogs, and Internet resources are examples of the technological advances utilized by these literary librarians. Jean Johnson described librarians as people who " . . . keep up with new trends in technology."[45] Librarians' commitment to the integration of new technologies into the provision of service has a history in which the profession can justifiably take pride.

The existence of books about libraries which make little to no mention of librarians is a thought-provoking phenomenon. Though four books out of thirty-five is a small percentage, the fact that such titles were published at all indicates that at least some people perceive that the materials in a library collection are more important than the people who provide the services. Perhaps the viewpoint that enables such books to be written and published helped to create the situation in which a book titled *We Need Librarians*[46] has a market.

The findings in the studies done to date must be interpreted with caution, because it is clear that there are many more books which should be studied. Subject searches suggest that OCLC's WorldCat lists over two hundred relevant titles and RLIN's Eureka shows one hundred. Careful bibliographical research would identify and locate the materials needed for a comprehensive examination of the treatment of librarians in children's literature.

DIRECTIONS FOR FURTHER RESEARCH

Many fruitful avenues exist for study of the cultural history of librarianship using children's literature as source material. A greater number of more extensive studies, using larger numbers of titles, should be done to verify or question the conclusions reached in the projects to date. Bibliographical research should be done so that scholars can easily access the titles needed for comprehensive study. Children's literature could be studied for evidence of attitudes toward libraries, as well as toward librarians, and comparisons made. Librarians as seen in children's literature could be compared to the depictions of librarians in fiction for adults.[47] Extensive, historically-based examinations of sub-genres of juvenile literature, such as picture books or career guides, could yield more insight into changing perceptions of the field. Technological change could be charted by a focused examination of the illustrations and descriptions of library tools and machinery. The backgrounds of the authors could be studied and comparisons made between materials written by librarians and by non-librarians. The trends noted in children's literature could be compared to data about the profession during the various decades, and to milestones in the history of librarianship to identify discrepancies and similarities.

CONCLUSION

This examination of thirty-five children's books from throughout the twentieth century revealed librarians who are positive, caring, energetic, and professional. The results suggest that library patrons may see librarians as librarians hope to be seen. These books provide evidence that the integration of new technologies into improved library service is a time-honored piece of the heritage of librarianship. The study reveals strong evidence that efforts to diversify the profession are still needed. Children's literature can and should be used to do more research into the cultural history of librarianship.

NOTES

1. R. Gordon Kelly, "Introduction," in *Children's Periodicals of the United States* (Westport, Conn.: Greenwood Press, 1984), x-xvi.

2. Norman D. Stevens, "Books about Us for Kids," *American Libraries*, October 1996, 52-53.

3. Norman D. Stevens, "A Review Article: Librarians and Libraries for Children," *Library Quarterly* 69, no. 1 (1999): 90-93.

4. Katherine M. Heylman, "Librarians in Juvenile Literature," *School Library Journal*, May 1975, 25.

5. Jill E. Buie, "The Image of the Librarian in Children's Literature" (Graduate research project, College of Library and Information Science, University of South Carolina, 1997).

6. Mary Ellen Davis, "The Portrayal of Librarianship in Literature Intended for Children, Preschool Through Third Grade" (Master's thesis, University of Wyoming, 1991), 9-11.

7. Ruby Othella Denman, "Librarianship as Revealed in Seven Recent Teen-Age Career Books" (Master's thesis, Texas State College for Women, 1954).

8. Virginia McNeil Speiden, "The Image of the Librarian as Seen in Eight Library Career Novels" (Master's thesis, University of North Carolina, 1961).

9. *Children's Catalog* (New York: H. W. Wilson Co., 1939-76).

10. Carolyn Mott and Leo B. Baisden, *The Children's Book on How to Use Books and Libraries* (New York: Charles Scribner's Sons, 1948).

11. C. R. Graham, *The First Book of Public Libraries* (New York: Franklin Watts, 1959).

12. Pekay Shor, *Libraries and You* (Englewood Cliffs, N.J.: Prentice-Hall, 1964).

13. Jeanne B. Hardendorff, *Libraries and How to Use Them* (New York: Franklin Watts, 1979).

14. Helen Ferris & Virginia Moore, *Girls Who Did: Stories of Real Girls and Their Careers* (New York: E. P. Dutton & Co., 1927).

15. Helen Ferris & Virginia Moore, *Girls Who Did: Stories of Real Girls and Their Careers* (New York: E. P. Dutton & Co., 1927).

16. Lucile F. Fargo, *Marian-Martha* (New York: Dodd, Mead & Co., 1936).

17. Katharine Ruth Ellis, *The Wide-Awake Girls in Winsted* (Boston: Little, Brown, 1909).

18. C. R. Graham, *The First Book of Public Libraries* (New York: Franklin Watts, 1959).

19. Lucinda Landon, *Meg Mackintosh and the Mystery in the Locked Library* (Boston: Little, Brown, 1993).

20. Jane Scoggins Bauld, *We Need Librarians* (Mankato, Minn.: Pebble Books, 2000).

21. Jeanne B. Hardendorff, *Libraries and How to Use Them* (New York: Franklin Watts, 1979), 36.

22. Marilyn Berry, *Help Is on the Way for Library Skills* (Sebastopol, Calif.: Living Skills Press, 1985), 32. Gail Gibbons, *Check It Out! The Book about Libraries* (San Diego: Harcourt Brace Jovanovich, 1985). Jean Johnson, *Librarians A to Z* (New York: Walker & Co., 1988), [4].

23. Roxie Munro and Julie Cummins, *The Inside-Outside Book of Libraries* (New York: Dutton Children's Books, 1996), [33-36].

24. Jane Scoggins Bauld, *We Need Librarians* (Mankato, Minn.: Pebble Books, 2000).

25. Mary Rebecca Lingenfelter, *Books on Wheels* (New York: Funk & Wagnalls, 1938).

26. Naomi Buchheimer, *Let's Go to the Library* (New York: G. P. Putnam's Sons, 1957).

27. Anne Rockwell, *I Like the Library* (New York: E. P. Dutton & Co., 1977).

28. Carmen Agra Deedy, *The Library Dragon* (Atlanta: Peachtree, 1994).

29. Mary Rebecca Lingenfelter, *Books on Wheels* (New York: Funk & Wagnalls, 1938).

30. Adele de Leeuw, *With a High Heart* (New York: Macmillan, 1945).

31. C. R. Graham, *The First Book of Public Libraries* (New York: Franklin Watts, 1959).

32. Edith Busby, *Behind the Scenes at the Library* (New York: Dodd, Mead & Co., 1960). Carla Greene, *I Want to Be a Librarian* (Chicago: Children's Press, 1960).

33. Jeanne B. Hardendorff, *Libraries and How to Use Them* (New York: Franklin Watts, 1979).

34. Roxie Munro and Julie Cummins, *The Inside-Outside Book of Libraries* (New York: Dutton Children's Books, 1996).

35. Adele de Leeuw, *With a High Heart* (New York: Macmillan, 1945).

36. Diane McClymont, *Books* (Ada, Okla.: Garrett Educational Corp., 1991).

37. Roxie Munro and Julie Cummins, *The Inside-Outside Book of Libraries* (New York: Dutton Children's Books, 1996).

38. Ann McLelland Pfaender, *Miss Library Lady* (New York: Julian Messner, 1954), 87.

39. Carmen Agra Deedy, *The Library Dragon* (Atlanta: Peachtree, 1994).

40. Katharine Ruth Ellis, *The Wide-Awake Girls in Winsted* (Boston: Little, Brown, 1909), 34.

41. Diane McClymont, *Books* (Ada, Okla.: Garrett Educational Corp., 1991), [25].

42. Pekay Shor, *Libraries and You* (Englewood Cliffs, N.J.: Prentice-Hall, 1964), 66.

43. Mary Ellen Davis, "The Portrayal of Librarianship in Literature Intended for Children, Preschool through Third Grade" (Master's thesis, University of Wyoming, 1991), 9-11.

44. Katherine M. Heylman, "Librarians in Juvenile Literature," *School Library Journal* (May 1975): 25.

45. Jean Johnson, *Librarians A to Z* (New York: Walker, 1988), [37].

46. Jane Scoggins Bauld, *We Need Librarians* (Mankato, Minn.: Pebble Books, 2000).

47. See Grant Burns, *Librarians in Fiction: A Critical Bibliography* (Jefferson, N.C.: McFarland, 1998).

BIBLIOGRAPHY

Baker, Donna. *I Want to Be a Librarian*. Chicago: Children's Press, 1978.

Bartlett, Susan. *A Book to Begin on Libraries*. New York: Holt, Rinehart and Winston, 1964.

Bauld, Jane Scoggins. *We Need Librarians*. Mankato, Minn.: Pebble Books, 2000.

Berry, Marilyn. *Help Is on the Way for Library Skills*. Sebastopol, Calif.: Living Skills Press, 1985.

Bonners, Susan. *The Silver Balloon*. New York: Farrar Straus Giroux, 1997.

Buchheimer, Naomi. *Let's Go to the Library*. New York: G. P. Putnam's Sons, 1957.

Buie, Jill E. "The Image of the Librarian in Children's Literature." Graduate research Project, College of Library and Information Science, University of South Carolina, 1977.

Burns, Grant. *Librarians in Fiction: A Critical Bibliography*. Jefferson, N.C.: McFarland, 1998.

Busby, Edith. *Behind the Scenes at the Library*. New York: Dodd, Mead & Co., 1960.

Children's Catalog. New York: H. W. Wilson Co., 1939-76.

Daly, Maureen. *Patrick Visits the Library*. New York: Dodd, Mead & Co., 1961.

Davis, Mary Ellen. "The Portrayal of Librarianship in Literature Intended for Children, Preschool through Third Grade." Master's thesis, University of Wyoming, 1991.

Deedy, Carmen Agra. *The Library Dragon*. Atlanta: Peachtree, 1994.

de Leeuw, Adele. *With a High Heart*. New York: Macmillan, 1945.

Denman, Ruby Othella. "Librarianship as Revealed in Seven Recent Teen-Age Career Books." Master's thesis, Texas State College for Women, 1954.

Ellis, Katharine Ruth. *The Wide-Awake Girls in Winsted*. Boston: Little, Brown & Co., 1909.

Fargo, Lucile F. *Marian-Martha*. New York: Dodd, Mead & Co., 1936.

Feehan, Patricia E. and Jill E. Buie. "Looking Up: The Image of Youth Services Librarians." *North Carolina Libraries*, Winter 1998, 141-44.

Felt, Sue. *Rosa-Too-Little*. Garden City, N.J.: Doubleday & Co., 1950.

Ferris, Helen and Virginia Moore. *Girls Who Did: Stories of Real Girls and Their Careers*. New York: E.P. Dutton & Co., 1927.

Gibbons, Gail. *Check it Out! The Book about Libraries*. San Diego: Harcourt Brace Jovanovich, 1985.

Ginther, Pemberton. *Miss Pat and Her Sisters*. Philadelphia: John C. Winston Co., 1915.

Graham, C. R. *The First Book of Public Libraries*. New York: Franklin Watts, 1959.

Greene, Carla. *I Want to Be a Librarian*. Chicago: Children's Press, 1960.

Hardendorff, Jeanne B. *Libraries and How to Use Them*. New York: Franklin Watts, 1979.

Heylman, Katherine M. "Librarians in Juvenile Literature." *School Library Journal*, May 1975, 25.

Johnson, Jean. *Librarians A to Z*. New York: Walker & Co., 1988.

Kelly, R. Gordon. *Children's Periodicals of the United States*. Westport, Conn.: Greenwood Press, 1984.

Landon, Lucinda. *Meg Mackintosh and the Mystery in the Locked Library*. Boston: Little, Brown & Co., 1993.

Levy, Elizabeth. *Something Queer at the Library: A Mystery*. New York: Delacorte Press, 1977.

Lingenfelter, Mary Rebecca. *Books on Wheels*. New York: Funk & Wagnalls, 1938.

McClymont, Diane. *Books*. Ada, Okla.: Garrett Educational Corp., 1991.

The Magic of Books: An Anthology for Book Week. New York: Dodd, Mead & Co., 1929.

Mott, Carolyn and Leo B. Baisden. *The Children's Book on How to Use Books and Libraries*. New York: Charles Scribner's Sons, 1948.

Munro, Roxie and Julie Cummins. *The Inside-Outside Book of Libraries*. New York: Dutton Children's Books, 1996.

Pellowski, Michael. *Ghost in the Library*. Mahwah, N.J.: Troll Associates, 1989.

Pfaender, Ann McLelland. *Miss Library Lady*. New York: Julian Messner, 1954.

Provines, Mary Virginia. *Bright Heritage*. New York: Longman, Green & Co., 1939.

Radlaver, Ruth Shaw. *Molly at the Library*. New York: Simon & Schuster, 1988.

Rockwell, Anne. *I Like the Library*. New York: E. P. Dutton & Co., 1977.

Saver, Julia L. *Mike's House*. New York: Viking Press, 1954.

Shor, Pekay. *Libraries and You*. Englewood Cliffs, N.J.: Prentice-Hall, 1964.

Speiden, Virginia McNeil. "The Image of the Librarian as Seen in Eight Library Career Novels." Master's thesis, University of North Carolina, 1961.

Stevens, Norman D. "Books about Us for Kids." *American Libraries*, October 1996, 52-53.

———. "A Review Article: Librarians and Libraries for Children." *Library Quarterly* 69, no. 1 (1999): 90-93.

Taylor, Mildred. *How to Write a Research Paper*. Palo Alto, Calif.: Pacific Books, 1974.

POPULAR PERCEPTIONS

Looking at the Male Librarian Stereotype

Thad E. Dickinson

SUMMARY. The library profession is haunted by stereotypes. Perpetually raising its infamous head is the portrayal of librarians as drab spinsters peering over the rim of their glasses and ready to "shush" a library patron for the offense of talking too loudly. It is an image that was born at the beginning of the twentieth century, and persists, albeit considerably diluted, to this day. On the other hand, positive and negative images of male librarians are to a large extent either ignored or treated very lightly in popular culture, especially in motion pictures and television. Once the exclusive domain of men, American librarianship evolved over the centuries to not just incorporate women, but to embrace and become almost completely associated with them. Stereotypes of male librarians have existed since colonial times; yet, the stereotypes have undergone considerable transformation as a result of professional and societal changes. This article attempts to understand some of the older stereotypes surrounding male librarianship in the United States by examining the position of the early librarian and the environment in which he worked. Current portray-

Thad E. Dickinson is Public Services Librarian, Nestle Library, School of Hotel Administration, Cornell University, Ithaca, NY 14850 (E-mail: ted26@cornell.edu).

[Haworth co-indexing entry note]: "Looking at the Male Librarian Stereotype." Dickinson, Thad E. Co-published simultaneously in *The Reference Librarian* (The Haworth Information Press, an imprint of The Haworth Press, Inc.) No. 78, 2002, pp. 97-110; and: *The Image and Role of the Librarian* (ed: Wendi Arant, and Candace R. Benefiel) The Haworth Information Press, an imprint of The Haworth Press, Inc., 2002, pp. 97-110. Single or multiple copies of this article are available for a fee from The Haworth Document Delivery Service [1-800-HAWORTH. 9:00 a.m. - 5:00 p.m. (EST). E-mail address: docdelivery@haworthpress.com].

10.1300/J120v37n78_07

als of male librarians in motion pictures and television are then discussed. The focus of this article is on academic male librarians; however, general male librarian stereotypes and issues are also discussed. *[Article copies available for a fee from The Haworth Document Delivery Service: 1-800-HAWORTH. E-mail address: <docdelivery@haworthpress.com> Website: <http://www.HaworthPress.com> © 2002 by The Haworth Press, Inc. All rights reserved.]*

KEYWORDS. Male librarians, librarianship–history, steretypes, popular culture

INTRODUCTION

It is no secret that a notable body of professional library literature is devoted to stereotypes and images of librarians. Personality tests, studies, and surveys go to great lengths to examine or repudiate the image of librarians in popular culture. By and large the image most often associated with and most often scrutinized by librarians is that of the female librarian. This is reasonable enough considering the majority of librarians are, in fact, women: in 1998, 79% of public librarians were women, while 69% of academic librarians were women.[1] Stereotypical images of male librarians also have their place in popular culture, but with much less frequency and, perhaps, with less vehemence. Nonetheless, the stereotypes exist and have done so for much longer than their female counterparts. Librarians in colonial America were primarily academic librarians and exclusively male, and remained as such until the last half of the nineteenth century. During this time period stereotypes of the "typical" academic male librarian found fodder to grow. When librarianship as a profession began to undergo the changes that characterize it as it is today, the image of male librarians naturally experienced change as well. Despite the many positive changes that have occurred, current stereotypes and images of male librarians still retain elements of the past.

EARLY ACADEMIC LIBRARIANS

Jody Newmyer writes that prior to 1870, the "prevailing assumption" was that librarians were "grim, grouchy, eccentric, and *male*,"[2] while Arnold Sable notes that an enduring caricature of early male librarians consisted of a "bibliophile, a pale, undernourished man who lived only for his books."[3] Exactly how such stereotypes came into existence and how prevalent they were in the early history of librarianship is unknown; however, a brief examination of early librarianship may provide some insight. The history of librarianship in the United States has its beginnings in colonial America with the founding of Harvard College in 1636. Thirty years would pass, however, before an individual was appointed to the library in any official capacity: Samual Stoddard became "Library Keeper" in 1667, effectively becoming America's first librarian. Stoddard remained as Harvard's librarian for about three years before moving on to pursue a career behind the pulpit, and was succeeded by Samual Sewell, who would later become a chief justice. Sewell's tenure was even shorter than Stoddard's, and it was not until 1672 that the Harvard College library finally appointed an individual who did not leave the position for another occupation. James Winthrop made a career as Harvard's librarian, remaining in the position for fifteen years, and is considered to be America's first professional librarian.[4] Other colonial colleges such as William and Mary, Yale, and Princeton eventually appointed library keepers of their own, a few of which garnered notable attention. Princeton's president, for instance, also served as the college "librarian" and eventually spearheaded the development of his library's first catalog,[5] while Yale's library encountered early difficulties when library keeper Daniel Buckingham, possibly displaying the "eccentric" aspect of the librarian stereotype, refused to turn over the collection that was destined for New Haven.[6]

Of particular importance in understanding how early male librarian stereotypes might have been born or perpetuated is realizing that the responsibilities and duties of the American colonial librarian were few in number and far from glamorous. When Stoddard was appointed librarian in 1667, Harvard's trustees established a set of "Library Laws" that directed Stoddard in the proper running and maintenance of the library. Library hours were from 11am-1pm daily; loan periods did not exceed one month; and books or items of great value were loaned out only in special circumstances and with extreme care.[7] Borrowing privileges were given only to professors, unless upon approval of the College President.[8] Certainly the restrictive nature of such library laws did not help to promote a positive image of the library keeper. Compounding those restrictions was the fact that many of the library keepers were required, once a month, to see to the return of all library books for inventory purposes and to assess damages.[9] In fact, it was not uncommon for the library laws to require that the librarian "make good" financially for all books unaccounted for at the end of his tenure.[10] Such library laws required that the library keeper restrict access to the collection, and it certainly behooved him to enforce them.

The work performed by early librarians likely contributed to their negative public image as well. Records indicate that the Harvard library keeper often participated in the student admission process; yet, in most cases, the early American librarian contented himself with sweeping the library floor, dusting and arranging the books, and airing the library once a week.[11] Reference or instructional services were nonexistent at this time. Virtually every library had closed stacks until well into the nineteenth century, making access to the collection by anyone other than the library keeper extremely unlikely. Collection development for the early librarians was primarily in the form of gifts to the library, although in later years fundraising was often added to the library keeper's duties.[12] It was also not uncommon for the library keeper to be in the unenviable position of collecting circulation fees and enlisting support from students. "Library Keeper" was essentially a custodial role that would remain virtually undisturbed into the next century, the implications of which would last well into the twentieth century.

The status of early librarians remains unclear. On one hand, historian Louis Shores writes that appointing a college librarian in colonial America came only after "deliberate considerations" since such an appointment was "considered of college-wide import."[13] There were no full-time librarians until Harvard's Winthrop, so professors or lessor instructors were often appointed to the position on a part-time basis, and, likewise, it was not uncommon for college presidents to assume the library keeper duties. In addition to Princeton's, the presidents at William and Mary, Yale, Harvard, Brown, King's (Columbia), and Dartmouth all carried out the duties of Library Keeper; tasks, Shores asserts, that were not inferior to a professor or president's other responsibilities. It is also interesting to note that several of the men who once held the position of Library Keeper would eventually achieve significant prominence in colonial America.[14] On the other hand, some scholars suggest that early librarians either did not have any particularly prominent status to begin with or that it declined over time. Orvin Shiflett writes: "The position of the librarian in the classical college . . . until the last quarter of the nineteenth century was a minor one. There was little or no feeling on the part of college officers that any special qualifications were necessary in the person chosen as librarian."[15] Shiflett further argues that professors who served as librarians did so "as a part of [their] natural duties," such as teaching and administrating, and if no professor could find the time to be the librarian, it was not unreasonable to find "a student, a janitor, or an unemployed clergyman" to serve in the position.[16] Apparently, just demonstrating a measure of responsibility was enough to be librarian in the first half of the nineteenth century. Although professors often assumed the duties of the librarian, the position was not at all comparable with that of teaching, so when the approach to higher education in the early nineteenth century began to emphasize more teaching and instruction on the part of professors, library hours and duties were curtailed, subsequently leading to less visibility and, perhaps, diminished status.[17]

In light of what has been written about the work and status of the early American librarians, Newmyer's stereotype, at least, does not seem too biased. Students in those days had to contend with librarians who were held financially accountable for missing books, who were often responsible for collecting fines and dues, and who were most likely already over-burdened professors.

THE BEGINNINGS OF REFERENCE SERVICE

Higher education in early nineteenth century America centered on instruction, the prevailing method being the use of a textbook and the lecture or recitation. Research was rarely conducted by professors themselves, much less required of students, and only found practice in the hands of "gifted amateurs" working independently of the colleges and at their own expense.[18] This approach to education and research in the United States would last until the last quarter of the nineteenth century, when what is known as the "research movement" was born in 1876 with the founding of Johns Hopkins University.[19] Harvard and other colleges soon followed. Drawing on the research and instruction traditions of the German universities, Johns Hopkins promoted graduate work and research as being as instrumental to higher education as instruction, and advocated the inseparability of research and instruction. By the end of the nineteenth century, research and scholarship went from being the work of "gifted amateurs" to being regarded as integral to the mission of American higher education.[20]

The resulting changes that took place in American higher education were revolutionary and few institutions and positions within the college benefited as much as the library and, theoretically at least, the librarian. The role of the college library in the early and mid-nineteenth century differed little from its role in the previous century; however, the changes ushered in by the research movement increased the need for larger collections and increased access, lifting the college library from its relative obscurity.[21] Coinciding with the changes taking place in academic libraries was a movement within public libraries that placed greater emphasis in aiding readers in the use of the library and in the selection of materials. The "public library movement" gave definition to the term "reference work," which involved providing occasional and limited assistance to library patrons.[22] Prior to either the research or public libraries movements, providing library assistance to the college student or professor "represented a distraction from the librarian's important duties . . . Cast in the role of the keeper of books, he [the librarian] was naturally inclined to regard the needs of the reader with indifference, if not hostility."[23] Two classic, albeit unflattering, portraits of mid-nineteenth century male college librarians can be found in accounts of John Langdon Sibley and Beverly Robinson Betts. Librarian at Harvard from 1856 to 1877, "Sibley was primarily a collector and conservator. He took little interest in casual readers and had no tolerance for the abuse of materials or infraction of rules."[24] Despite his enormous contributions to Harvard's collection, Sibley is best known to library history for his supposed response to Harvard President Charles W. Eliot's inquiry into Sibley's excited and determined purpose one day: all the books were safely in the library except two, and he was on his way to retrieve them.[25] Sibley appears to characterize the stereotype described by Sable, while accounts of Columbia's Betts find a remarkable resemblance to Newmyer's "grim, grouchy, eccentric, and *male*" image. Describing Columbia's library in 1876, a professor wrote of Betts: " . . . [He] crept up to the building about eleven o'clock in the morning . . . He seemed generally displeased when anyone asked for a book and positively forbidding when asked to buy one."[26] Melvil Dewey, lauded as librarianship's most esteemed innovator, was appointed librarian after Betts' tenure ended. It is possible that these accounts of Sibley and Betts were isolated and unfair, but the fact that their image as librarians was so negative could only have given strength to existing librarian stereotypes.

Fortunately, many academic librarians began to follow the lead of the public libraries. In *College Library Administration*, published in 1876, Rutgers librarian and mathematics instructor, Otis H. Robinson, strongly advocates an educational role for librarians: "A brief course of lectures on books; how to get them; how to keep them, and how to use them, would come from a scholarly librarian in a systematic way with much better effect than desultory talks from the head of different departments."[27] Robinson argues that the librarian is responsible for assisting in the investigation of a subject; whereas, an instructor might provide a list of books to his student, the librarian instructs the student on how to locate and use the information. "He [the student] wants not results but a method."[28] At Columbia College, Dewey put theory into practice and employed two reference librarians by 1885, eventually organizing the Reference Department the following year.[29] Dewey's reference model at Columbia was not immediately accepted at a number of academic libraries, one barrier being the then long held belief by faculty and librarians alike that a researcher did not need the help of librarians. Similarly, some librarians believed that the catalog was sufficient in itself to lead readers to the material. It was enough, for example, that the library novice, generally a student, was given "artful and limited instruction in the use of the library" and then usually left to fend for himself.[30] By the end of the nineteenth century, however, most academic librarians recognized the development of reference services as central to the mission of the library and the librarian. Interestingly, Harvard, the birthplace of American librarianship, did not have an official reference department until 1915.[31]

WOMEN IN ACADEMIC LIBRARIES

Another revolution taking place during the mid- and late nineteenth century, the consequences of which would greatly impact the image of male librarians, was the introduction of women into the American work force. The second half of the nineteenth century saw an increase in educational opportunities for American middle-class women, especially at the collegiate level, and the professions most welcoming to the college graduates were teaching and librarianship. Prior to this time, librarianship was considered "a man's job."[32] Christine Williams theorizes that increased immigration to the United States forced "native-born single women" to leave their factory jobs, which then allowed more women to get an education and pursue a position in libraries.[33] Indeed, demands placed on American libraries as a result of the public library and research movements required a larger, educated workforce. The Boston Public Library was the first library to hire women, employing them as library clerks in 1852, while the Boston Athenaeum hired America's first woman librarian in 1857.[34] Shortly thereafter, Harvard College Library became the first academic library to hire women when it began doing so in 1858.[35] Libraries were quick to hire these women because they generally worked for lower wages than their male counterparts, and the work assigned to them was almost certainly the dull and more routine tasks that once filled the male librarian's day. Kenneth Carpenter describes the work that women performed in libraries as being "at the lowest level. They were not even heads of small libraries . . . The first women employees of libraries were hired to do low-level work in institutions headed by men."[36] Employing women in libraries was also viewed by many as a natural extension of the supposedly inherent feminine qualities of spirituality, housekeeping, and a willingness to help others.[37] It is argued that one result of women accepting these low-level positions was the creation of a profession where men, though in the minority, held most of the higher salaried, administrative positions within America's libraries, a contentious issue to this day and well beyond the scope of this article.

Although the pace of entry and recognition for women in libraries remained slow, by 1870, 43 of the 213 librarians in the United States were women, and when the American Library Association convened for its first conference in 1876, 11 percent of the attendees were women.[38] Dewey significantly influenced the entry of women into academic libraries when, in 1883 as Librarian in Chief at Columbia, he hired six Wellesley College graduates, or the "Wellesley half-dozen," as library assistants, and later, when he founded America's first library school at Columbia in 1887. Of the 20 members of that first class, 17 were women.[39] By the turn of the century, women comprised 75 percent of all librarians in the United States.[40]

MEN IN A FEMINIZED PROFESSION

Carpenter writes that there was not some "golden age of male librarianship," that came to an end;[41] yet, what had once been a "man's job" in which "men were everywhere"[42] was by the turn of the century completely associated with women. The resulting "feminization" of librarianship also feminized many of the male librarian stereotypes. Newmyer's "grim, grouchy, eccentric, and *male*" stereotype and Sable's "bibliophile, a pale, undernourished man who lived only for his books" were largely replaced by the "kindly and sometimes effeminate misfit,"[43] and "weak and non-masculine individuals."[44] Understanding the nature behind these stereotypes begins with recognizing that when women began seeking employment outside of the home, long established societal roles were threatened. "The rise of feminism," Passet explains, "and the movement of women from the home to the school and workplace contributed to a 'blurring of boundaries and overlapping of gender spheres.' "[45] The masculinity of librarians was never an issue when libraries were wholly the realm of men, but by the beginning of the twentieth century the societal concept of masculinity was redefined in such a way that made male librarians suspect. This perception of librarianship as a "woman's job" also tended to adversely influence a man's willingness to become a librarian, subsequently limiting the number of men in the profession. Men of that era tended to consider librarianship as better suited for women than men, and the man pursuing a career as a librarian could easily be perceived as having failed at the more traditional male occupations. A man might feel his identity and status as a man compromised by choosing to become a librarian.[46] Rader Hayes writes that men who choose to enter professions dominated by women are considered "irrational" by others outside of the profession, and are very often seen as being unqualified for a position in a traditionally male occupation.[47] Although there is little evidence that male librarians actually gave up their positions because librarianship had become feminized, it is likely that most men no longer considered librarianship as a potential career.

There was also little financial incentive for a man to become a librarian. Salaries for librarians were known to be very low, especially in comparison with traditionally male occupations, and men as the generally accepted "breadwinners" of a family in the nineteenth and early twentieth centuries were not likely to choose a career that might cast doubt on their ability to be providers.[48] Whether the low salaries were the result of the predominance of women in librarianship or society's low regard for the profession remains debatable. It is generally accepted, however, that the low salaries significantly influenced a man's decision not to become a librarian.

Men who did enter into librarianship often sought administrative positions not only because the salaries were larger, but also because subordinate positions such as reference librarian were thought to lack the intellectual rigor that characterized the male-dominated professions of law and medicine.[49] The male academic librarian stereotype reflected how society perceived a man in a female-dominated profession, as ". . . a broken down man who failed in other lines of work."[50] Recruitment of men into non-administrative library positions remained low throughout much of the first half of the twentieth century. Following World War II, recruiting efforts by universities, the American Library Association, and library schools strongly targeted men in hopes of creating more of a balance between the number of men and women in librarianship, but low salaries and a poor public image continued to deter men from pursuing the non-administrative positions.[51] Librarianship itself suffered from a stereotype that cast it as "weak, dependent, conservative, and nonintellectual."[52] Recruiting literature in the 1940s then began promoting the library profession to men by emphasizing a steady income, job security, and "community respect."[53] The 1950s did see an increase in the number of men entering the field, although it is likely the incentive to do so centered more on the opportunities for administrative advancement than any other factor. Later recruiting efforts would remain hamstrung by salary and prestige issues, but it is reasonable to suggest that the stereotypes of male librarians as "effeminate misfit[s]" and "weak and non-masculine" played an even larger role in turning men away from academic librarianship.

MODERN IMAGES OF THE MALE LIBRARIAN

Stereotypical images of male academic librarians in the last quarter of the twentieth and the first years of the twenty- first century appear to have shed much of the "non-masculine" characteristic. How American society has redefined masculinity can certainly be credited with helping to change the stereotype. There is also the possibility that male librarians themselves had an influence. Sable writes: "The male librarian wants first, before proving himself a librarian, to prove himself as a male. He does not want to be considered as belonging to the female stereotype."[54] Of course, the possibility remains that such stereotypes never really found strong footing in the public consciousness. In the early 1990s, a study conducted by James Carmichael, Jr., found that the image of the effeminate or gay male reference librarian was more entrenched within the library profession itself than it was outside of it.[55] In fact, images of male academic librarians are so rare in the overwhelmingly popular and influential mediums of motion pictures and television as to be virtually nonexistent.

In his work, *The Celluloid Librarian: The Portrayal of Librarians in Motion Pictures*, William King notes only four male librarian roles in the seventeen films he researched. Of those four roles, only one is considered a major role; two are married; and two are portrayed negatively.[56] Academic libraries are apparent in only two of the seventeen films, but there is no indication that the librarians in those films are male or female. Ann O'Brien and Martin Raish published a later (1993) filmography of 126 films that included 104 films not mentioned in King's work. Male librarians and library assistants appear in only 11 of those films, and there are no indications that academic libraries are featured in any of the 11 films. Still, despite the low numbers of male librarians in general, Raish hints that the male librarian characters do resemble past stereotypes, often being portrayed as "failed 'something elses,' or are too dreamy and vague to hold down a real job."[57] In *Something Wicked This Way Comes*, for example, the librarian played by Jason Robards, Jr. is described as "a meek librarian with some dark secrets and regrets,"[58] while the unpleasant male librarian portrayed in *Sophie's Choice* harkens back to Columbia College's "positively forbidding" Betts. Beth Yeagley's *Shelving, Stamping and Shushing: Librarians in the Movies* reviews 28 films, of which 21 were released after Raish's filmography was published. Yeagley's study further supports how infrequently academic librarians are portrayed in motion pictures: only 4 academic librarians are portrayed out of the 28 films reviewed,[59] but their gender is not specified. Nonetheless, Yeagley's study does indicate an overall improvement in the portrayal of male librarians as a whole.

With a few exceptions, there are virtually no current studies or literature on the portrayal of librarians, let alone male librarians, in television. Certainly librarians have been portrayed in situation comedies, dramas, family-oriented programs, and commercials, and it would no doubt be a daunting task, considering the huge number of television shows and characters; still, it is an area that warrants investigation. Two popular television series that have portrayed male librarians are *Seinfeld* and *Buffy the Vampire Slayer*. In the *Seinfeld* episode, "The Library," Lt. Bookman, though not an actual librarian but a "library investigator," personifies many of the older male librarian stereotypes such as "grim, grouchy" and extremely zealous about the return of library books. In contrast to the character of Lt. Bookman is *Buffy the Vampire Slayer*'s, Rupert Giles. GraceAnne A. DeCandido describes Giles as "elegant," "handsome," and "charged with eroticism."[60] Although the Giles character is not an academic librarian, he does break the male librarian mold by engaging in the traditionally un-librarian position of helping to slay vampires and other evils; he is a "hero-librarian." Yet, Giles can also be seen portraying some of the male librarian stereotypes; DeCandido calls him "technologically inept," "occasionally befuddled," and "tweedy."[61] Giles, writes John Cullen, "is a Luddite working in a field that is reliant on information technology. He is self-absorbed and unhelpful . . . He has no concept of reader service and is always surprised when students enter the library to do real research."[62]

CONCLUSION

Stereotypes, Pauline Wilson remarks, "all seem to be resistant to change. Some may be impossible to change."[63] In the case of male librarians, Wilson is partially correct. Colonial and early American librarians were stereotyped as severe and indifferent, while the later nineteenth century portrayed academic male librarians as physically weak and consumed with books and order. When the twentieth century was in its infancy, male librarians in general began to be perceived by society at large as feminine failures. Today, academic male librarians do not figure too much in modern popular culture, but male librarians in general still endure portrayals in film and television that carry over attributes from the past, while at the same time incorporating newer, fresher characteristics. In almost every instance it can be seen that the stereotypes associated with male librarians reflect the work environment and job duties of the librarians: when the work was dull, so were the stereotypes; when librarianship became feminized, male librarians were cast as such; and as societal norms and technology evolved, so has the perception of librarians outside of the profession. More portrayals of academic male librarians in such mediums as television and film are necessary to promote the diversity of librarianship, and although the stereotypes are unlikely to disappear, the history of male librarianship seems to hint that as the library profession continues to change, so will the stereotypes, but for the better.

REFERENCES

1. Lynch, Mary Jo. "What We Know About Librarians." *American Libraries* 31, no. 2 (February 2000): 8-9.

2. Newmyer, Jody. "The Image Problem of the Librarian: Femininity and Social Control." *Journal of Library History* 11, no. 1 (January 1976): 44-67.

3. Sable, Arnold P. "The Sexuality of the Library Profession." *Wilson Library Bulletin* 43, no. 8 (April 1969): 748-751.

4. Hamlin, Arthur T. *The University Library in the United States: Its Origins and Development.* Philadelphia: University of Pennsylvania Press, 1981, p. 11.

5. Shores, Louis. *Origins of the American College Library: 1638-1800.* New York: Barnes and Noble, Inc., 1953, p. 141.

6. Ibid., 24

7. Zubatsky, David. *The History of American Colleges and Their Libraries in the Seventeenth and Eighteenth Centuries: A Bibliographical Essay.* Champaign, IL: University of Illinois, Graduate School of Library Science, 1979, p. 24.

8. Shores, 181-182.

9. Ibid., 146.

10. Zubatsky, 24.

11. Shores, 140, 202.

12. Holley, Edward G. "Academic Libraries in 1876." *College and Research Libraries* (January 1976): 15-47.

13. Ibid., 140.

14. Shores, 140-141.

15. Shiflett, Orvin Lee. *Origins of American Academic Librarianship.* Norwood, NJ: Ablex Publishing Corporation, 1981, p. 45.

16. Ibid., 46.

17. Ibid., 34.

18. Rothstein, Samuel. "The Development of Reference Services through Academic Traditions, Public Library Practice and Special Librarianship." In "Rothstein on Reference . . . With Some Help from Friends." *The Reference Librarian*, nos. 25/26 (1989): 33-155.

19. Ibid., 36.

20. Ibid., 38.

21. _____. "An Unfinished History: A Developmental Analysis of Reference Services in American Academic Libraries." In "Rothstein on Reference . . . With Some Help from Friends." *The Reference Librarian*, nos. 25/26 (1989): 365-409.

22. Rothstein *Unfinished*, 373.

23. _____. "The Development of the Concept of Reference Service in American Libraries, 1850-1900." *The Library Quarterly* 23, no. 1 (January 1953): 1-15.

24. Hamlin, 27.

25. Holley, 15.

26. Hamlin, 43. Quoting J.W. Burgess, *Reminiscences of an American Scholar*, 74-75.

27. Robinson, Otis H., "College Library Administration." In *Public Libraries in the United States of America.* Washington: U.S. Bureau of Education, 1876, p. 521.

28. Ibid., 522.

29. Rothstein *Concept*, 10-11.

30. Rothstein *Unfinished*, 374.

31. Rothstein *Academic Traditions*, 86.

32. Sable, 748.

33. Williams, Christine L. *Still a Man's World: Men Who Do "Women's Work."* Berkeley: University of California Press, 1995, p. 25.

34. Schiller, Anita M. "Women in Librarianship." In *The Role of Women in Librarianship, 1876-1976: The Entry, Advancement, and Struggle for Equalization in One Profession*, edited by Kathleen Weibel, Kathleen M. Heim, and Dianne J. Ellsworth. Phoenix, AZ: The Oryx Press, 1979, p. 237.

35. Hamlin, 119.

36. Carpenter, Kenneth E. (1996). A Library Historian Looks at Librarianship. *Daedalus* [Online], 77, 11 pp. Available: Dow Jones Interactive [2000, August 21].

37. Schiller, 238-239.

38. Ibid., 237.

39. Passet, Joanne E. "Men in a Feminized Profession: The Male Librarian, 1887-1921." *Libraries and Culture* 28, no. 4 (Fall 1993): 385-402.

40. Schiller, 237-238.

41. Carpenter, 3.

42. Sable, 748.

43. Morrisey, Locke J., and Donald O. Case. "There Goes My Image: The Perception of Male Librarians by Colleague, Student, and Self," *College and Research Libraries* 49 (1988): 454, quoting Allan Angoff, "The Male Librarian-an Anomaly," *Library Journal* 84 (February 1, 1959): 553.

44. Beaudrie, Ronald, and Robert Grunfeld. "Male Reference Librarians and the Gender Factor." *The Reference Librarian* no. 33 (1991): 211-213.

45. Passet, 385.

46. Hayes, Rader. "Men's Decisions to Enter or Avoid Nontraditional Occupations." *The Career Development Quarterly* 35, no. 2 (December 1986): 89-101.

47. Ibid., 89-90.

48. Ibid., 90.

49. Passet, 387.

50. Passet, 392.

51. O'Brien, Nancy P. "The Recruitment of Men into Librarianship, Following WWII." In *The Status of Women in Librarianship: Historical, Sociological, and Economic Issues.* Edited by Kathleen M. Heim. New York: Neal Schuman Publishing, 1983, p. 62.

52. Newmyer, 44.

53. O'Brien, 56.

54. Sable, 751.

55. Carmichael, James V., Jr. "Gender Issues in the Workplace: Male Librarians Tell Their Side." *American Libraries* 25, no. 3 (March 1994): 227-230.

56. King, William H. "The Celluloid Librarian: The Portrayal of Librarians in Motion Pictures." Master's thesis, University of North Carolina at Chapel Hill, 1990.

57. O'Brien, Ann, and Martin Raish. "The Image of the Librarian in Commercial Motion Pictures: An Annotated Filmography." *Collection Management* 17, no. 3 (1993): 61-84.

58. Ibid., 66.

59. Yeagley, Beth. "Shelving, Stamping, and Shushing: Librarians in the Movies." Master's thesis, Kent State University, 1999.

60. DeCandido, GraceAnne A. "Bibliographic Good vs. Evil in 'Buffy the Vampire Slayer.'" *American Libraries* 30, no. 8 (September 1999): 4 pp. Online. InfoTrac. *Expanded Academic ASAP.* March 26, 2001.

61. Ibid.

62. Cullen, John. "Rupert Giles, the Professional-Image Slayer." *American Libraries* 31, no. 5 (May 2000): 1 p. Online. EBSCOhost. *Academic Source Elite.* 3072684. April 28, 2001.

63. Wilson, Pauline. *Stereotype and Status: Librarians in the United States.* Westport, CT: Greenwood Press, 1982, p. 4.

Know-It-All Librarians

Beth Posner

SUMMARY. Librarians are depicted as know-it-alls by some and as
know-nothings by others. Similarly, they are seen as both utterly powerless and preternaturally powerful. This essay offers examples of these
contradictory images, examines their implications, and proposes a more
realistic view of librarians and their relation to knowledge and power. *[Ar-
ticle copies available for a fee from The Haworth Document Delivery Service:
1-800-HAWORTH. E-mail address: <docdelivery@haworthpress.com> Website:
<http://www.HaworthPress.com> © 2002 by The Haworth Press, Inc. All rights
reserved.]*

KEYWORDS. Librarians' image, knowledge, power

INTRODUCTION

One image of librarians is that they are know-it-alls who can answer
any question. This image–sometimes consciously or unconsciously
promulgated by librarians, themselves–may also be held by knowledge
seekers who are new to the world of information or intimidated by its
pursuit. To them, librarians can seem like magicians who occupy a
rarified space in which answers are always at their disposal. From this
perspective, librarians control access to information and have the power
to provide assistance, but will only do so *if* they happen to be interested
in the question and in a good mood. More often, they are presumed to be
too intellectually arrogant to be either helpful or interested.

Beth Posner is Interlibrary Loan/Reference Librarian, Mina Rees Library, CUNY
Graduate Center, 365 Fifth Avenue, New York, NY 10016 (E-mail: bposner@gc.
cuny.edu).

[Haworth co-indexing entry note]: "Know-It-All Librarians." Posner, Beth. Co-published simultaneously
in *The Reference Librarian* (The Haworth Information Press, an imprint of The Haworth Press, Inc.) No. 78,
2002, pp. 111-129; and: *The Image and Role of the Librarian* (ed: Wendi Arant, and Candace R. Benefiel) The
Haworth Information Press, an imprint of The Haworth Press, Inc., 2002, pp. 111-129. Single or multiple copies of this article are available for a fee from The Haworth Document Delivery Service [1-800-HAWORTH,
9:00 a.m. - 5:00 p.m. (EST). E-mail address: docdelivery@haworthpress.com].

10.1300/J120v37n78_08

At the same time, given that library work encompasses everything from the sublime and the complex to the banal and the ridiculous, a rival image of librarians also exists. In this view, library work requires little effort or intelligence and librarians must be prodded, pushed, or provided with a breadcrumb trail in order to track down even the most routine request. Since many common questions answered at reference desks are not very challenging–for instance, "Where is the bathroom?" or "How much does a photocopy cost?"–some see librarians as little more than worker bees or drones who occupy the gray world of the unimaginative and uninspired. Particularly, today, when so many have so much information at their fingertips, librarians can appear increasingly unimportant and powerless.

It is the common Western tendency towards the binary that makes dichotomous thinking–and dichotomous images such as these–so common. It *is* often simply easier to classify things as black or white than it is to decide and describe which of the infinite shades of gray they may be. However, one useful aspect of the postmodern project–and one purpose of this article–is to point out the simplifications and other misleading implications that come from framing issues in terms of opposites, whether the opposites are us-other, master-slave, civilized-uncivilized, or librarians as know-it-alls or know-nothings, omnipotent or powerless.

As knowledge workers, exactly how librarians are perceived with respect to knowledge and power is of particular importance. What they know and do not know are essential aspects of both their self-image and the image that others will have of them. And, if, as Francis Bacon noted, "knowledge, itself, is power," then their knowledge base is directly related to what librarians do and do not have the power to do. Of course, the relation of knowledge to power is a complicated one.[1] But, whatever the exact relation, knowing a subject means understanding and applying facts and methods in order to harness power to achieve relevant goals. So, in order for librarians–through the knowledge and practice of library science–to reach any of the goals that they have for patrons, libraries, or themselves, then the boundaries of what they know and do not know must first be established.

IMAGE: "THE KNOW-IT-ALL LIBRARIAN"

We called him Mr. Know-All, even to his face. He took it as a compliment.

–Somerset Maugham, Mr. Know-All[2]

The idea of knowing it all, or of omniscience, has long had an influence on "scientific and philosophical thought, and more generally [on] images of knowledge, nature, history and of humanity."[3] Contemporary theologians explore religions that portray their supreme being(s) as possessing complete knowledge of the past, present and future, while philosophers examine omniscience in relation to epistemology. In literature, it is authors and narrators who may be omniscient, and in psychology, omniscience is discussed in connection to both infant development–where it is short-lived and healthy, and psychoses–where it is far more entrenched and unhealthy.

A variety of other characters–such as parents, psychoanalysts, doctors, leaders, and various experts–are also sometimes considered to be virtually omniscient. Still, most theorists consider omniscience too extreme a concept to be very useful. Surely, it is a sign of insanity for any human to believe that they know it all, and perhaps, even, as Debra Castillo observes:

> One of the major features of the insane mind . . . consists of the way it knows. . . . The madman . . . seeks to assimilate whatever he encounters into his frame of reference, without ever truly recognizing or acknowledging any new fact. . . . It is only in this sense that the mad librarian can be said to know at all.[4]

However, although reaching or even approaching omniscience is impossible–or possible only in God, authors or the insane–it is also a concept that offers insight into certain characters, particularly certain librarians, whose ego ideal is to be knowledgeable. As Janette Caputo observes, "the librarian who satisfies every user's request without delay [and] with totally accurate information . . . is a fantasy of first semester library school students."[5] This is fantastic because practical considerations of time and resources, the standards of the library profession, and the nature of knowledge, itself, limit a librarian's ability to respond to informational requests. Yet, despite all this, some librarians hold on to this particular semi-functional delusion of intellectual grandeur throughout their careers and lives.

Examples of know-it-all librarians exist in both contemporary and historical literature, as well as in both popular and library literature. In only the second issue of *Library Journal*, published in 1876, we read that,

> A librarian should not only be a walking catalogue, but a living cyclopedia. . . . Librarians . . . are expected to know everything; and in a sense they should know everything–that is, they should have that *maxima pars eruditionis*, which consists in knowing where everything is to be found.[6]

Similar points of view are also expressed in non-library literature. One hundred years ago, *The London Times* printed the view that "the ideal librarian must be a man of rare and almost superhuman gifts."[7] And, today, Erica Joyce Olsen's website proclaims, "People become librarians because they know too much . . . Librarians are all-knowing and all-seeing."[8]

Images of know-it-all librarians can also be found in non-library literature. In the 1995 film *Party Girl*, the librarians act intellectually superior to Mary, the clerk, in part because they know how a library works and she–at first–does not. In Jorge Luis Borges' short story, "Library of Babel," the universe is envisioned as a library containing every possible book. There, people are called "imperfect librarians" because no one can find books with correct answers among the multitudes that exist. This implies that a perfect librarian would be able to do so, and indeed, there is one alleged librarian, "the Man of the Book," who is analogous to God, because having found the book that explains it all, he knows it all.

Mystery novels regularly feature librarians as crime solvers because of how much they know and how adept they are at finding answers. [9] In Umberto Eco's *The Name of the Rose*, an intellectually glorified image of librarians is evident in the hubris of those who "corrected the errors of nature"[10] by shelving books according to where their authors should have been born, rather than where they actually were born. Another example is seen when William, the monk who solves the murder mysteries is told, "What a magnificent librarian you would have been . . . you know everything."[11] Although well aware of the dangers of knowledge, he is also something of a know-it-all–exceedingly proud and sure of his learning, reasoning and empirical skills.

Now that we have seen examples of this image, let us turn our attention to how and why it developed. One hundred years ago, John Ashhurst explained the way a librarian might come to a posture of omniscience. The librarian, he said,

> . . . is treated with a certain amount of deference, he finds that he is able to answer many questions that puzzle little boys and old la-

dies without having to have recourse to reference books, his staff laugh politely at his jokes, and after a time he finds that he is probably more familiar with the titles and names of the authors of a greater number of book than about anyone of his acquaintance . . . He grows so accustomed to the appearance of his books on the shelves . . . [that] he really comes to feel as if he must have read them. . . . But the real downfall of a librarian . . . probably dates from the time when he first discovers a mistake in the writings of some well-known authority.[12]

Additionally, when a librarian, through a good reference interview or years of experience, understands what a patron needs even better than that person knows or can articulate, and can immediately find whatever information is needed, an impressed patron's awe might well become exaggerated, as, in turn, might the librarian's self-image.

Perhaps some librarians choose to perpetuate this particular stereotype because they are inflicted with so many negative stereotypes, while this is one that feeds something positive in them. As Katherine Adams explains, there is something enjoyably subversive and empowering about claiming a stereotypical image as one's own.[13] In addition, delighting patrons with their knowledge is not only pleasurable for both librarians and patrons, but can also bring librarians needed prestige and financial support from patrons. Or, alternatively, perhaps it is because some librarians do not understand the real and certain value of their work and knowledge that they feel the need to inflate their self-importance by acting like know-it-alls.

There are even professors of library science and other librarians who teach–or at least imply–that a good reference librarian can find the answer to any question. In reality, however, a number of researchers have found that only 55 percent of reference questions are answered accurately.[14] This "55% rule" is a highly contested statistic,[15] but if it is acknowledged that librarians answer at least some questions incompletely, if not incorrectly, then it must be attitude,[16] more than ability, that fuels the image of librarian as know-it-all.

As understandable as the enjoyment of this image may be, and as important as knowledge is to librarians and society, knowing it all is still not an unequivocally positive image for librarians–or anyone–to maintain. Warnings about the risks of too much knowledge abound. Children are told that "no one likes a know-it-all" and entertaining a delusion of grandeur, such as omniscience, is considered to be a clear sign of psychological dysfunction. It is a desire for more knowledge that leads to the fall of Adam and Eve from the Garden of Eden, and it is partly due to a desire to know it all that Faust sells his soul to the devil. In *The Name of the Rose*, the Devil is described as "truth that is never seized by doubt"[17] and "the trouble in the abbey came from those who knew too much not too little."[18] Even Plato condemned the poet as "a charlatan whose apparent omniscience is due entirely to his own inability to distinguish knowledge and ignorance."[19] Though less severe, know-it-alls who finish your sentences or give away the endings of movies are still quite annoying, and know-it-all librarians can even do harm to themselves and others.

The American Library Association Code of Ethics[20] states that librarians should be courteous to patrons. If, instead, a person is faced with a know-it-all librarian with a bad attitude, they may not only leave the library without answers . . . they may be emotionally devastated, as well. This occurs in *Sophie's Choice*, when Sophie goes to the library to find the poems of Emily Dickinson but mistakenly asks for those of the American poet, Emile Dickens. The librarian, assuming that she means Charles Dickens, insists that everyone knows that he was not American and did not write poetry. His attitude, accompanied by her own frailties, rattles her so badly that she faints.[21] A know-it-all librarian may not even deign to explain things to people who do not know as much as they do–or think they do. People regularly apologize to librarians because they think theirs is a "stupid question." So, if librarians want people to come to them with their informational needs, they must not only make clear what questions they can answer, they must also convince people that they are approachable and interested in any and all queries.

The existence of this image–and even a slight belief in it by librarians–can also be harmful to librarians, themselves. Acting like a know-it-all is a defense against fears of uncertainty, and it can become pathological if it is used to avoid self-knowledge and its attendant difficulties.[22] If someone is sure that they know what is and is not possible, instead of questioning and thinking things through, they may cease to experience reality or make any effort.[23] When faced, as all inevitably will be, with something that they do not know or cannot adequately explain, a librarian who expects to know everything will, at the least, get frustrated and irritable. While some amount of perfectionism may be necessary for libraries to function, if librarians irrationally believe that they must also be perfect, then they will worry too much about every question and problem, become unduly nervous, and make mistakes. No human being–librarians included–would want to live without the "emotions of wonder, adventure, curiosity and laughter"[24] that, as Santayana explained, omniscience excludes.

IMAGE: "SHELVERS-WITH-ATTITUDE"

No plant is able to think about itself or able to know itself . . . no plant can do anything intentionally . . . Its growth has no meaning, since a plant can not reason or dream . . . [Chauncey Gardner] . . . would be one of them.

–Jerzy Kosinski, *Being There*,[25]

Countering the image of librarians as know-it-alls is the view that they are know-nothings. Many people are shocked to discover that librarians are required to have a graduate degree (or two) for their jobs. To them, a librarian's only ability and desire–other than to hide out in libraries and be left alone–is to check items in and out, assess overdue fines, and "shush" library patrons.

Like the image of the know-it-all librarian, this stereotype is one that has existed throughout the history of librarianship. Over 125 years ago, librarians recognized that there were some among them who were untrained and simply not good at their jobs. They knew that there were " . . . corporators and civic councilors who conceive that the extent of a librarian's duties is to pass books over a counter . . . They say of us [we] have nothing to do and are fully equal to it."[26] And, even today, the "55 percent rule" may make some librarians feel as good–or as bad–as know-nothings.

Examples of know-nothing librarians exist in contemporary popular literature, as well. In *The Name of the Rose*, Malachi, the monastery's librarian, "seemed quite thoughtful, but on the contrary, he was a very simple man . . . he was a fool."[27] In the science fiction book, *Wyrms*, there is a character named Heffiji who is a librarian of sorts. Papers with answers written on them are scattered throughout her house, but they are not arranged in any systematic way. As she admits, "I don't know anything but I can find everything."[28] Of course, librarians do have organizing principles, but since most people do not understand them, they undoubtedly question their efficacy, if not their existence.

Nescience, the opposite of omniscience, "is a nostalgic, regressive, atavistic condition . . . it may be provisionally defined as the state of being unacquainted with a cultural archive (the textual embodiment of knowledge)."[29] Like omniscience, the idea of nescience is portrayed in the Bible when Adam and Eve are in a state of blissful ignorance until they eat from the Tree of Knowledge. Prior to that, although not as knowledgeable, they are closer to God, and it is precisely this sort of spiritual knowledge that is thought to derive more from nescience than omniscience. There is also a long history of anti-intellectualism that holds that too much concern with learning is bad for society and individuals,[30] and that oftentimes, action or acceptance are more productive than analysis. However, librarians are not mystics, nor–hopefully–are they anti-intellectuals, so nescience is not the sort of image they should do anything to encourage.

One reason that this image exists may be that librarianship has not been considered a profession for very long, and it quickly became a feminized one. Perhaps, as Penny Cowell says, an early "emphasis on housekeeping tasks performed in a fussy manner has trivialised library work."[31] Radford and Radford posit that libraries are symbols of order and that librarians control that order. Therefore, perhaps, in an effort to minimize people's fears of knowledge and discourse, librarians are "feminized" and made to appear as victims of this order rather than as rulers of it.[32] Or, perhaps librarians have acquired this image because they are in a service industry with little or no direct connection to the making of money, which is considered so important in our culture. Instead, their connection is to bookishness, which seems to be less and less respected. (Similarly, other knowledge workers, such as computer scientists, may be more respected, because their work and image is so much more connected to profit making and computers than to books and education.)

Some would-be-patrons, know-it-alls themselves, assume that everyone else knows less than they do, if not nothing. Others, intimidated by libraries, overwhelmed by information, and misunderstanding what libraries can provide, may downplay the abilities of librarians in order to make themselves feel better. Many businesses, and even schools, consider the library to be merely a support service, akin to a typing pool. Similarly, some see all library workers as clerks, instead of distinguishing librarians as professionals with education, duties and abilities beyond what they can see. (For instance, while librarians may be developing collections by studying book reviews, patrons only see them sitting around and reading magazines.) Perhaps, because people think that anyone can type keywords into a computer and get an answer, they are unimpressed by what it is that librarians appear to do at work. Or, perhaps it is because librarians work in places that others use for leisure or education that they are not considered particularly professional or capable.

There are also those who think that librarians know nothing about the real world because they are always reading, rather than living. They simply assume that librarians prefer the company and knowledge of books to the company of people and the knowledge of life. This is Marion the Librarian's mother's viewpoint in *The Music Man*. She does not expect anyone to listen to her daughter, given that Marion is more concerned with her library than with finding a husband, and by extension, a life in the real world. Even some librarians, in the early years of *Library Journal*, expressed a similar point, repeatedly using the phrase "the librarian who reads is lost." It is true that empirical knowledge–which comes from experience–must be supplemented by analysis, because no one can experience everything first-hand, and even when people do engage in direct observation, their senses can be deceived. However, it is also true that sometimes, the more one intellectualizes, the further one can get from knowledge that is directly relevant to the real world. Both reading and living are, therefore, profitable exercises from which librarians can learn a great deal.

REALITY: WHAT LIBRARIANS KNOW

Since neither of these extremes portrays an accurate image of what librarians know, let us now consider just what knowledge they do possess.

- *Librarians know how to find information*. As Samuel Johnson noted, "Knowledge is of two kinds–we know a subject or we know how to find information on it," and one definition of knowledge is "the ability to produce the correct answer to a question."[33] This, first and foremost, is what librarians know.
- *Librarians know how to collect, preserve, organize, and dispense information*. Knowledge can also be defined as understanding acquired through experience or study. The responsibility of librarians, with respect to the economy of knowledge, is to know how to collect, preserve, organize and dispense information for that study.
- *Librarians know how to get things done*. In addition to their process and subject knowledge, librarians have practical knowledge. They can fix copy machines and printers, load microfilm machines,

raise and budget money, and manage all of the everyday aspects of their work.

- *Librarians know how to work with people.* It is a librarian's job to bring people and information together, thus encouraging the creation and transmission of knowledge. This means that as much as they know about information, they must also know about people. From knowing how to conduct reference interviews and determine what information a person needs, to knowing how to calm someone facing a deadline and a broken copy machine, a librarian's understanding of people is essential.

- *Librarians know what information literacy means and how to impart information literacy skills to others.* Librarians know–and can explain to others–how, done properly, the review and consideration of existing information saves time and opens people up to new ideas, insights and understandings. (It also indicates what is already known so that efforts can be focused on applying and testing information or on answering other questions.) Despite their prejudices towards research, however, librarians also know, and must teach others, that scholarship can, and often does, proceed without the use of secondary "library" sources. Indeed, independent thinking may even be stifled and overwhelmed when confronted with too much pre-existing data. Although librarians have always served as conduits between people and information, research studies[34] and experience at reference desks indicates that many people do not understand that a librarian's job is to help answer their questions. So, people need to be taught to ask for help. Also, librarians know that not all information is reliable, so as they teach people how to find information, they must teach them how to evaluate what they find.

- *Librarians know how to work with electronic information.* As even the smallest libraries get connected to the Internet and all that it encompasses, no librarian can know their entire collection. And, even if they did, online catalogs, databases, indexes, and research engines could also–quickly, cheaply and reliably–tell people what is available. However, since technological interfaces are not always user-friendly and the actual content of such services is sometimes lacking, a librarian's knowledge of how to handle computerized data is much needed.

- *Librarians know about the nature of knowledge and its limits.* Despite all the well-considered wisdom of sages and scholars throughout time, and the massive accumulation of information in libraries and computer databases, librarians know that questions not only remain . . . they proliferate. Given that knowledge is relative and human understanding finite and biased, questions and problems are simply a natural, intrinsic and inevitable part of life. No amount of information will answer everything and some information will even lead to more problems than it solves. Thus, problems will always exist, but so will more fortunate byproducts, such as hope and determination (and plenty of jobs for librarians).

- *Librarians know how other limits they face–such as a lack of resources–effect what they can do.* With so much information in existence, there is always more to be acquired, and each acquisition comes with additional costs. Most libraries do not have the money or space they need, nor do cataloging systems have the breadth they need to fully encompass everything. Librarians know what this means in terms of what they can provide to patrons, and they also know how to make the system work within these limits.
- *Librarians know how knowledge and information are connected.* The interconnectedness of knowledge makes interdisciplinary research important, and when people need to work outside of their fields, they are especially likely to need the help of librarians. This interconnectedness also means that, to a certain extent, it is an unnecessary redundancy for researchers or librarians to know or have to look at everything. So, librarians must understand these connections in order to decide what their libraries will provide and how to guide patrons to the most relevant material.

IMAGE: "DRAGON LIBRARIANS" OR MEEK, WEAK, GEEKS

Just as knowledge and power are related, so are omnipotence and omniscience, and as such, they are often considered together. The same characters who are regularly judged omniscient–parents, psychoanalysts, doctors, leaders, authors, and God–are often deemed omnipotent, as well. This connection can also be seen in the use of the word *authority*. Not only does knowledge makes someone an authority, but being an authority gives people power and the right to use it to accomplish their ends.

To become healthy adults, we all need to realize the limits of our power. However, human development also includes an acquaintance with the feeling of omnipotence; through good parenting, infants are given a taste of being all-powerful, which in turn helps them learn that they are real.[35] A librarian, however, may experience this feeling as an adult, too. When in charge of a reference desk or library, with all the information that they have at their fingertips, librarians can actually feel like absolute rulers of their own little fiefdom. As Alison Hall says, "Librarians, it would seem, have the potential for immense power . . . by withholding, or alternatively, disseminating knowledge."[36]

However, despite the idea that knowledge is power and that a librarian's mastery of information can provide them with strong feelings of control, it is interesting that librarians are generally perceived of as meek, rather than strong, and as thinkers–and not great thinkers, at that–rather than doers. Perhaps, because they seem so quiet at work, they are assumed to be weak and ineffectual. Or, perhaps, it is because the standards of their profession guide them not in the use of information, but in providing information for others to use that they are seldom considered powerful.

Still, despite all this, images of mighty librarians do exist. We know that Batgirl was, indeed, a librarian, and Spider Robinson describes one of his characters, Mary Kay Kare, as "one of the secret masters of the world: a librarian. They control information. Don't ever piss one off."[37] Jet Li, in the movie, *Black Mask*, plays a mild-mannered librarian who enjoys the peace of the library, but is also a super-powerful superhero. And, in Sean McMullen's *Soul in the Machine*, not only are there Dragon Librarians who routinely fight duels, but two of the most powerful warrior-rulers in the world are librarians. As Erica Olsen's riff on the Internet ends, "Librarians wield unfathomable power. . . . Librarians rule. And they will kick the crap out of anyone who says otherwise."[38]

REALITY: WHAT LIBRARIANS CAN DO

Librarians who feign knowledge or ignorance, or strength or weakness–becoming either pseudo-intellectuals or mere paper pushers–will find it difficult to do their jobs successfully. And, patrons who over-estimate the abilities of librarians will be frustrated when their expectations are not met, while those who underestimate the capacities of librarians will never ask for their help. Either way, there will be disappointment and unmet information needs, and as a result, people may completely turn away from libraries and librarians. Should they do this, getting information from unreliable sources or doing without information that they really do need, then the impact is potentially quite dire, not only for the future of librarianship but also for those individuals and society.

Complicating the issue is the fact that all of these contradictory images exist at the same time, both in the minds of librarians and in the minds of others. Entrenched images are difficult to dispel, but nonetheless, librarians have the power to do many things that can help people understand just what it is that librarians know and can do. Specifically,

- *Librarians can study their image(s).* It seems that librarians have always been interested in and concerned with the image of their profession. But, the old focus on bemoaning and challenging stereotypes is now also being supplemented by a postmodern call to deconstruct, understand, subvert and sometimes even embrace them. Either way, understanding various aspects of an image is the first step towards embracing or combating it. Coupled with a dispassionate, even ironic, assessment of one's self and others, librarians can determine why they are viewed in a certain way, what this means to themselves and to others, and what they might do in order to successfully project a more positive and realistic image.
- *Librarians can tell people what they know, what they do not know, and why.* Every person a librarian meets, in the library or outside of it, provides them with an opportunity to confront their images. Although it can be easier to fall into expected behaviors, librarians will only grow personally and professionally if they present themselves as they really are. And, although librarians cannot control the way others view them, they can control the way they present themselves. Every person they help learns what they know and every person they cannot help learns what they do not know. So, while distinguishing themselves as librarians, they should always clearly and openly explain how it is that they know some things and why it is that they do not know others.
- *Librarians should not be know-it-alls.* In order to act at all, librarians should never think of themselves as know-it-alls. An omniscient being "is never presented with options, never enjoys the capacity to acquire intentions, and is unable to act intentionally [so] far from being 'free' to choose and act, or unlimited in power, it is, of necessity, omni-impotent."[39] Those who think they already know it all will never try to change or improve themselves. And, certainly, this is not an image librarians will ever disabuse others of, if they believe it themselves.

- *Librarians should not think of others as omniscient or of themselves as know-nothings.* Believing that others know it all–or always know more than they do–leads people to abdicate personal responsibility and rely too much on what those others think. Librarians who assume that information scientists or publishers, deans or library board members know more than they, are doing a disservice both to themselves and their patrons. In this, the "information age," it is time that librarians acknowledge their areas of expertise and take more visible leadership roles in the larger world.

- *Librarians can study epistemology and the changing nature of information.* Library science education should include more instruction about the philosophical basis of epistemology,[40] so librarians will truly understand what knowledge is, what it can do, and how it may be changing. Computer technology, for instance, has made information less fixed (as books are) and more fluid, changeable and relativistic.[41] Only librarians who understand the changing nature and power of information can work out what this implies for the nature of knowledge and its use.

- *Librarians can teach people about the limits of information technology, as it exists today.* Some people think that libraries offer them no more, and often less, than what they can find on any computer. That they will miss important sources, or take more time than necessary to find them, may not even occur to them. Or, if it does, they still may not turn to a librarian for help because they do not think librarians *can* help. In some ways, it may feel like a relief to librarians when people learn to use electronic databases by themselves and when troublesome patrons stay at home and logon to library databases through proxy servers, instead of demanding attention at the library. True, librarians might then have more time to do other work, but without some sort of contact with people–whether face-to-face or remote–librarians lose valuable opportunities to help and show people what they know and can do.

- *Librarians can be more proactive in helping people search for knowledge and information.* In some ways, the traditional professional standards of library science limit what librarians can or will do for people. Reference librarians were originally so-named because they simply referred people to books.[42] It was only later that their job description came to include finding information for people and/or teaching them how to find it for themselves. Today's *ALA Guidelines for Behavioral Performance of Reference and In-*

formation Services Professionals state that one goal of librarianship is to make people information literate and self-sufficient by imparting research strategies, not answers,[43] so most librarians still will not retrieve or evaluate information for people. However, with more and more information being generated, librarians need to advise people more and organize knowledge better in order to keep information overload to manageable proportions. Otherwise, information overload, in the extreme, may just lead to information impotence.

- *Librarians can fight against unnecessary limits.* Librarians must consciously decide which, among the limits that exist, to accept and which, with proper effort, they can transcend. Cuts in acquisitions budgets or limits in new building space translate into real problems, not only for librarians but for patrons and society, as well. So, if librarians do not fight for what they need in terms of budgets, schedules, etcetera, then needed resources will be directed to louder–and not necessarily more worthy–advocates.

- *Librarians should accept necessary limits.* It is human nature to struggle against limits, and many successes have certainly come from this struggle. Still, although binary thinking makes it easier sometimes to accept nothing when one cannot have it all, it is only by recognizing realistic limits that librarians can concentrate on knowing and doing what is possible and most productive. While innovations and discoveries regularly increase the world's bounty, there is just no alchemy that can increase certain basic resources; infinite amounts of anything–including knowledge–are just not seen in everyday life. And, even when certain limits can be transcended, a conscious decision should be made as to whether the costs of doing so are acceptable ones. As people and resources are pushed harder and harder, care must be taken that no one and nothing is pushed beyond the breaking point. If this is not done, then by trying to continually get more for less, or by trying to be everything to everyone, librarians may use up too many resources and too much of themselves.

- *Librarians can support and trumpet more complicated and realistic depictions of themselves in fiction and in the media.* One way to dispel an image is to replace it with a stronger one. Library associations have run advertising campaigns that focus on what *libraries* do, but they should also use their media savvy to depict what *librarians* know and do. Depictions of well-rounded, realistic librarians in movies, popular novels or television shows are also helpful. Some particularly well written fictional librarians, who know a great deal, but definitely not everything, include Bunny Watson, in the movie *Desk Set*, Mary, in the movie *Party Girl*, Jan O'Deigh, in Richard Powers' award winning bestseller, *The Goldbug Variations*, and Rupert Giles, from the television show *Buffy: The Vampire Slayer*.

Ultimately, the more that librarians know and do, the more power they will have to help people meet their information needs. And, whatever librarians may or may not know, there is no doubt that their sustained attempts to answer all questions and their continual efforts to organize and make available all information are invaluable to knowledge building. So, a better understanding of their relation to knowledge and power is a step not only towards a more realistic image of librarians, but also towards a better understanding of knowledge and power in a world where both are increasingly important.

NOTES

1. Budd, John. *Knowledge and Knowing in Library and Information Science*. MD: Scarecrow Press, 2001.

2. Maugham, Somerset. *The Complete Short Stories of W. Somerset Maugham*. NY: Doubleday, 1952: 144.

3. Ceruto, Mauro. *Constraints and Possibilities: The Evolution of Knowledge and the Knowledge of Evolution*. Switzerland: Gordon and Breach Science Publishers, SA, 1994: 28.

4. Castillo, Debra. *The Translated World: A Postmodern Tour of Libraries in Literature*. Tallahassee: University Presses of Florida, 1984: 47.

5. Caputo, Janette S. *The Assertive Librarian*. AZ: Oryx Press, 1984: 28.

6. Smith, Lloyd. "The Qualifications of a Librarian." *The American Library Journal*, vol. 1, 1876: 70.

7. "The Ideal Librarian," *Library Journal* 7 (June 1882): 106.

8. Olsen, Erica. *Thwart not the librarian*. [Online.] Available: http://www.msu.edu/~olseneri/library.html.

9. Burns, Grant. *Librarians in Fiction: A Critical Bibliography*, NC: McFarland and Company, 1998: 4.

10. Eco, Umberto. *The Name of the Rose*. San Diego: Harcourt Brace Javonovich, 1983: 314.

11. Eco: 567.

12. Ashhurst, John. "On Taking Ourselves Too Seriously." *Library Journal*, May 1901: 268.

13. Adams, Katherine C. "Loveless Frump as Hip and Sexy Party Girl: A Reevaluation of the Old-Maid Stereotype." *The Library Quarterly*, vol. 70, no. 3, July 2000: 298.

14. Crowley, Terrence, "Half-Right Reference: Is It True?" *Reference Quarterly*, Fall 1985: 65.

15. Durrance, Joan C. "Reference Success: Does the 55% Rule Tell the Whole Story?" *Library Journal*, April 15, 1989: 35.

16. Jardine, Carolyn. "Maybe the 55% Rule Doesn't Tell the Whole Story: A User-Satisfaction Survey." *College and Research Libraries*, vol. 56, November 1995: 477.

17. Eco: 81.

18. Eco: 64.

19. Plato. *The Republic*. Harmondsworth: Penguin, 1967: 375.

20. American Library Association. *ALA Code of Ethics*. [Online.] Available: http://www.ala.org/alaorg/oif/ethics.html.

21. Styron, William. *Sophie's Choice*. NY: Random House, 1979: 10.

22. Bell, D.L. "Knowledge and Its Pretenders: Bion's Contribution to Knowledge and Thought," in *Psychosis: Understanding and Treatment*. ed. Jane Ellwood, London and PA: Jessica Kingsley Publishers, 1995: 81.

23. Eigen, Michael "Aspects of Omniscience," pp. 604-628 in *The Facilitating Environment: Clinical Applications of Winnicott's Theory*, eds. Fromm, M. Gerard and Smith, Bruce L. CT: International University Press, 1989: 608.

24. Santayana, *Realms of Bring*: xiii.

25. Kosinski, Jerzy. *Being There*. NY: Harcourt Brace Jovanovich, 1971: 3-8.

26. Winsor, Juston. "The Presidential Address." *Library Journal*, vol. 2, September 1877.

27. Eco: 420.

28. Card, Orson Scott. *Wyrms*. NY: Arbor House, 1987: 138.

29. Martin, Andrew. "The Genesis of Ignorance: Nescience and Omniscience in the Garden of Eden." *Philosophy and Literature*, vol. 5, 1981: 19.

30. Thiem, Jon. "The Great Library of Alexandria Burnt: Toward the History of a Symbol." *The Journal of the History of Ideas*, vol XL, 1979: 520.

31. Cowell, Penny. "Not All in the Mind: The Virile Profession." *Library Review*, vol. 29, 1980: 172.

32. Radford, Marie L. and Radford, Gary P. "Power, Knowledge, and Fear: Feminism, Foucault, and the Stereotype of the Female Librarian." *Library Quarterly*, vol. 67, no. 3, 1997: 259-260.

33. White, Alan. *The Nature of Knowledge*. NJ: Rowman and Littlefield, 1982: 119.

34. Durrance: 31.

35. Eigen: 605.

36. Hall, Alison. "Batgirl Was a Librarian." *Canadian Library Journal*, vol. 49, 1992: 345.

37. Robinson, Spider. *The Callahan Touch*. NY: ACE Books, 1993: 64.

38. Olsen: www.msu.edu/~olseneri/library.html.

39. Kapitan, Tomis. "Agency and Omniscience." *Religious Studies*, vol. 27, March 1991: 119.

40. Budd, John. *Knowledge and Knowing in Library and Information Science*. MD: Scarecrow Press, 2001.

41. Smith, Anthony. *From Books to Bytes: Knowledge and Information in the Postmodern Era*. BFI Pub., 1993.

42. Durrance: 33.

43. American Library Association. *ALA Guidelines for Behavioral Performance of Reference and Information Services Professionals*. [Online.] Available: http://www. ala.org/rusa/stnd_behavior.html.

REFERENCES

Adams, Katherine C. "Loveless Frump as Hip and Sexy Party Girl: A Reevaluation of the Old-Maid Stereotype." *The Library Quarterly*, vol. 70, no. 3, July 2000: 287-301.

American Library Association. *ALA Code of Ethics*. [Online.] Available: http://www. ala.org/alaorg/oif/ethics.html.

American Library Association. *ALA Guidelines for Behavioral Performance of Reference and Information Services Professionals*. [Online.] Available: http://www.ala. org/rusa/stnd_behavior.html.

Ashhurst, John. "On Taking Ourselves Too Seriously." *Library Journal*, May 1901: 265-268.

Bell, D.L., "Knowledge and Its Pretenders: Bion's Contribution to Knowledge and Thought," pp. 70-82 in *Psychosis: Understanding and Treatment*, ed. Jane Ellwood, London and PA: Jessica Kingsley Publishers, 1995.

Budd, John. *Knowledge and Knowing in Library and Information Science*. MD: Scarecrow Press, 2001.

Burns, Grant. *Librarians in Fiction: A Critical Biography*. NC: McFarland and Company, 1998.

Caputo, Janette S. *The Assertive Librarian*. AZ: Oryx Press, 1984.

Card, Orson Scott. *Wyrms*. NY: Arbor House, 1987.

Castillo, Debra. *The Translated World: A Postmodern Tour of Libraries in Literature*. Tallahassee: University Presses of Florida, 1984.

Ceruto, Mauro. *Constraints and Possibilities: The Evolution of Knowledge and the Knowledge of Evolution*. Switzerland: Gordon and Breach Science Publishers, SA, 1994.

Cowell, Penny. "Not All in the Mind: The Virile Profession." *Library Review*, 1980: 167-175.

Crowley, Terrence. "Half-Right Reference: Is It True?" *Reference Quarterly*, Fall 1985: 59-68.

Durrance, Joan C. "Reference Success: Does the 55% Rule Tell the Whole Story?" *Library Journal*, April 15, 1989: 31-36.

Eco, Umberto. *The Name of the Rose*. San Diego: Harcourt Brace Javonovich, 1983.

Eigen, Michael, "Aspects of Omniscience," pp. 604-628 in *The Facilitating Environment: Clinical Applications of Winnicott's Theory*, eds. Fromm, M. Gerard and Smith, Bruce L., CT: International University Press, 1989.

Hall, Alison. "Batgirl Was a Librarian." *Canadian Library Journal*, vol. 49, 1992: 345.

"The Ideal Librarian," *Library Journal*, vol. 7, June 1882: 106.

Jardine, Carolyn. "Maybe the 55% Rule Doesn't Tell the Whole Story: A User-Satisfaction Survey." *College and Research Libraries*, vol. 56, November 1995: 477-485.

Kapitan, Tomis. "Agency and Omniscience." *Religious Studies*, vol. 27, March 1991: 105-120.

Kosinski, Jerzy. *Being There*. NY: Harcourt Brace Jovanovich, 1971.

Martin, Andrew. "The Genesis of Ignorance: Nescience and Omniscience in the Garden of Eden." *Philosophy and Literature*, vol. 5, 1981: 3-20.

Maugham, Somerset. *The Complete Short Stories of W. Somerset Maugham*. NY: Doubleday, 1952.

Olsen, Erica. *Thwart not the librarian*. [Online.] Available: http://www.librarianavengers. com/library.html.

Plato. *The Republic*. Harmondsworth: Penguin, 1967.

Radford, Marie L. and Radford, Gary P. "Power, Knowledge, and Fear: Feminism, Foucault, and the Stereotype of the Female Librarian." *Library Quarterly*, vol. 67, no. 3, 1997: 250-266.

Robinson, Spider. *The Callahan Touch*. NY: ACE Books, 1993.

Santayana. *Realms of Bring*, xiii.

Smith, Anthony. *From Books to Bytes: Knowledge and Information in the Postmodern Era*. BFI Pub., 1993.

Smith, Lloyd. "The Qualifications of a Librarian." *The American Library Journal*, vol. 1, 1876: 69-74.

Styron, William. *Sophie's Choice*. NY: Random House, 1979.

Thiem, Jon. "The Great Library of Alexandria Burnt: Toward the History of a Symbol." *The Journal of the History of Ideas*, vol. XL, 1979: 507-526.

White, Alan. *The Nature of Knowledge*. NJ: Rowman and Littlefield, 1982.

Winsor, Justin. "The Presidential Address." *Library Journal*, vol. 2, September 1877.

Students' Perceptions
of Academic Librarians

Jody Fagan

SUMMARY. Academic librarians, eager to participate in the education of college students, have been researching library anxiety, students' aversion to asking questions, and other problems with interactions between students and library staff for decades. Misconceptions about librarians' professional status, teaching roles, knowledge and expertise, and attitudes toward students are often proposed as causes of dysfunctional interactions and as reasons why some students don't ask questions. It is important for students to know that librarians are willing and able to help, so that they feel free to ask questions that will help them advance their education. This study reports the findings of a survey of 48 undergraduate students regarding their perceptions of academic librarians, and discusses ideas for addressing existing misconceptions. *[Article copies available for a fee from The Haworth Document Delivery Service: 1-800-HAWORTH. E-mail address: <docdelivery@haworthpress.com> Website: <http://www. HaworthPress.com> © 2002 by The Haworth Press, Inc. All rights reserved.]*

KEYWORDS. Academic librarians, professional status, undergraduate students, librarianship, library jobs

Librarians have a long history of writing articles about their professional image (or lack thereof). Pauline Wilson describes fifty years of

Jody Fagan is Assistant Professor, Morris Library, Southern Illinois University, Carbondale, IL 62901 (E-mail: jfagan@lib.siu.edu).

[Haworth co-indexing entry note]: "Students' Perceptions of Academic Librarians." Fagan, Jody. Co-published simultaneously in *The Reference Librarian* (The Haworth Information Press, an imprint of The Haworth Press, Inc.) No. 78, 2002, pp. 131-148; and: *The Image and Role of the Librarian* (ed: Wendi Arant, and Candace R. Benefiel) The Haworth Information Press, an imprint of The Haworth Press, Inc., 2002, pp. 131-148. Single or multiple copies of this article are available for a fee from The Haworth Document Delivery Service [1-800-HAWORTH, 9:00 a.m. - 5:00 p.m. (EST). E-mail address: docdelivery@haworthpress.com].

literature about librarians' images of themselves, beginning in 1921.[1] In 1985, an *American Libraries* opinion survey sent to random ALA members showed 69.5% of respondents felt improving the public's perception of librarians was important, ranking image tenth in importance in a list of 32 items.[2] In 1990, Patricia Schuman suggested image concerns should not be about physical stereotypes, but about librarians' usefulness and necessity.[3] Image of librarians has even been measured by the Myers-Briggs Type Indicator twice in contradictory studies, once in the '70s and '80s by the Center for Applications of Psychological Type, and once in 1992 by the Association for College and Research Libraries.[4] Julie Still examined image and roles of librarians in subject-specific pedagogical literature in 1998, finding that although surveyed teaching faculty say libraries and librarians are important to higher education, this is not reflected in their literature.[5] The Popular Culture Association's 1999 annual conference included papers and presentations concerning librarians' image issues.[6] There have also been numerous short columns and humorous discussions on this topic in library magazines throughout the years.[7]

Studies specifically about student perceptions of academic librarians are rarer. Peter Hernon and Maureen Pastine's 1977 study was the most recent found in *Library Literature* at the time of writing that was specifically targeted at this topic.[8] Many authors have studied problems of which incorrect perceptions of academic librarians may be one cause, including library anxiety and fear of asking questions. For example, library anxiety seems to be a common problem among college students, and discomfort with seeking assistance from librarians seems to play a significant part in their anxiety.[9] Solutions proposed to solve this problem in the college setting often focus on changing students' perceptions of librarians, including improving interpersonal skills at the reference desk and adding more warmth to interactions with students, particularly in library settings.[10, 11]

Another significant problem that may result from incorrect perceptions of librarians is a fear of asking questions. Swope and Katzer found 65% of students with specific needs would not ask for assistance from a librarian, for these reasons:

- They did not want to disturb the librarian.
- They felt their questions were too basic.
- They were dissatisfied with the previous performance of the librarian.[12]

Jiao suggested these reasons indicate vague, inconsistent, and errone-
ous perceptions about libraries and library staff.[13]

Even if library users do not experience library anxiety and are comfortable asking questions, they may not seek help for other reasons. Perhaps they feel information-finding is an individual responsibility, or
perhaps they don't know there is expertise available to solve complex
information problems. Reaching non-users is important whether they
are uncomfortable or just misinformed; they all have information needs
with which an expert could help. Learning about their perceptions may
suggest what the obstacles actually are.[14] Misconceptions and lack of
knowledge about librarians may also result in a library's struggle to get
funding or other support. This article examines the results of a survey
about students' perceptions of academic librarians, and discusses ideas
for addressing the areas of misunderstanding.

RESEARCH GOALS AND OBJECTIVES

Since students may not actively think about their perceptions of librarians, surveys are a good way to get them to think and express their
unrealized opinions.

Hernon and Pastine's study was based on a questionnaire returned by
362 students and interviews with twenty of the students who had responded to the questionnaire. Although the study under discussion in
this article varies in methodology and scope from Hernon and Pastine's,
the two will be compared where relevant. The study centered around
three questions:

1. Do students perceive the role of librarians, clerical, or student assistants as being the same?
2. Do students perceive librarians as service rather than teaching oriented?
3. Do students believe that librarians do less than they actually do in
   terms of duties?[15]

Our study centered around four questions, which overlap Hernon and
Pastine's to some degree:

1. What education, knowledge, skills, and expertise do students
   think librarians have?
2. Do students know which workers in their library are librarians and
   what do students think librarians do?

3. Do students perceive librarians as valuable to their own work, and what role do they perceive librarians playing in their own education and to the University?
4. What is the student's perception of the librarian's attitude toward their jobs and toward helping students?

Although the results of this survey are useful for many avenues of further study, they will be used in particular to design and test a course module in a for-credit library class regarding the education, job duties, and attitudes of academic librarians. Students will then be asked to evaluate if knowing more about librarians changed their behavior when seeking help in the library.

THE SURVEY INSTRUMENT AND SETTING

Morris Library serves a campus of over 20,000 with more than 2 million volumes, 12,000 serial publications, and 24-hour study access, and employs 42 faculty and A/P staff and 85 civil service staff. Forty-eight undergraduate students in a one-credit introductory library skills class at Southern Illinois University returned a survey concerning their perceptions of academic librarians, which is included in Appendix A. Extra credit was given to those students who completed the survey. The one-credit course was titled "The Library as an Information Source" and was taught by professional librarians in an auditorium with a projected computer screen for demonstration purposes. Each semester includes two sections of the class with a maximum of 60 students per section.

The survey was constructed of 48 questions of various types, including 30 five-option continuum questions, nine Yes/No questions, six open-ended short answer questions, and three checklist questions. The data was sorted by both class and gender, by the frequency with which the student consulted an academic librarian, and by whether or not the student felt academic librarians helped them succeed in their education; however this correlational data is still under analysis. The survey noted that the phrase "academic librarians" referred to librarians who work in libraries at universities like SIUC.

RESULTS

Respondents were asked to identify their gender and class. Of the 48 respondents, 26 were female and 22 were male. Seven were freshmen,

10 were sophomores, 12 were juniors, 16 seniors, and 2 identified themselves as others.

In response to some aspects of the survey, students seemed ambivalent. The most popular response to the continuum questions was "Neither Agree Nor Disagree," and some students left many of the open-ended "list five things . . . " questions incomplete, even though they were instructed to complete them fully to receive extra credit points. Although undoubtedly some students were just doing sloppy work, most just seemed not to know what to write. In hindsight, the continuum questions should have featured a "Don't Know" column to allow respondents to express this bewilderment or ignorance.

Students' Perceptions Concerning the Education of an Academic Librarian

The survey asked what degree(s) students thought an entry-level librarian must have, with options ranging from "high school degree" to "multiple doctoral degrees." The majority (57%) checked "bachelor's degree," 28% checked either "high school degree" or "some college classes," and only 15% checked "master's degree." None chose doctoral degrees as a requirement.

The survey also asked respondents to list five topics they thought would be covered in library classes. Although a few respondents listed non-library school subjects such as math and English grammar, most of the topics listed were related to library work in some way. Most responses did not describe elementary tasks such as shelving, but described many of the professional aspects of the profession, such as "research of library systems" and "ways to set up a library." There were also a large number of responses related to technology, ranging from the simple ("computer skills") to the more complex ("internet applications in library technology"). Topics were not limited to reference functions but described a wide variety of library subjects, including classification, management, "laws of libraries," preservation, acquisitions, web development, and library history.

Hernon and Pastine's respondents were also unsure of the educational background of academic librarians. Most (87%) thought librarians differed from library assistants and library student workers in educational background, but only eight of their 362 respondents opined that academic librarians have master's degrees in library science.[16]

What Skills, Knowledge, and Expertise
Do Students Think Academic Librarians Have?

Our survey next asked respondents to list skills that librarians have that were valuable to them. Respondents referred most often to librarians' knowledge, particularly of where resources are located and of computers and the Internet. Although respondents frequently noted librarians' helpfulness in answering questions, finding materials was emphasized much more than *how* to use materials. A significant number of respondents also listed character qualities (e.g., "friendly") in answer to this question. Other major response groups included communication skills, organizational skills, and skills with the Internet and computers.

Most respondents acknowledged that librarians were much faster at figuring out tough questions and had knowledge that was practical to students. The majority also indicated that librarians helped them search the Internet more effectively, although they were unclear if librarians are "experts with technology."

Respondents were evenly split in answer to the question "Do you feel that academic librarians have helped you succeed in your college education?"

Although it gave no specific percentages, Hernon and Pastine's study found that many students did not feel academic librarians played an important role in their college education.[17]

The survey also asked respondents if librarians' skills were valuable to the University. Seventy-one percent of respondents said librarians were useful to the University in ways that don't directly relate to students. An open-ended question asked students to list five *skills* that were of value to the university, but respondents usually referred to *knowledge* that librarians had. Most responses described knowledge *about* topics (e.g., "knowledge of literature"), rather than knowledge of how to do things (e.g., "know how to use informational systems"). Significant groups of responses included knowledge about library materials (this group was the largest), help with research to faculty and students, organizational skills, skills related to improving the library (e.g., "form web pages for help"), ordering materials, and good communication skills. Character qualities were also suggested as reasons librarians were valuable, including "loyalty" and "open mind." Many respondents showed a lack of understanding of the professional nature of librarians, some suggesting that librarians "do excess teacher work" or "stay after and clean up."

Do Students Know Which Workers in Their Library Are Librarians and What Do Students Think Librarians Do?

About half of the respondents said they could tell which workers in Morris Library were librarians. The survey also asked respondents if they ever asked to speak to a librarian; 92% said no. Unfortunately, our survey did not ask students how they could tell which workers were librarians. However, the rest of the survey reveals at least some of the reasons for respondents' overwhelming negative response, including ignorance of a librarian's education, knowledge, and skills, and in some cases, misconceptions about librarians' attitudes.

Hernon and Pastine's respondents said they differentiated librarians from other staff because they were "older, sitting behind desks," and were "more knowledgeable and competent in their assistance." In Hernon and Pastine's study, 40.7% of respondents indicated they would ask for a librarian if they needed expertise.[19]

A majority (85%) of respondents in our study correctly identified academic librarians as faculty members at SIUC, and also correctly agreed that librarians had to do research like other faculty. Respondents were mixed (46% yes, 54% no), however, as to whether librarians were faculty at other universities. Seventy-nine percent of respondents thought an entry-level academic librarian would make $25,000 or less per year.

Our study also asked students to list five different job duties they thought librarians perform regularly. Although the wide range of responses covered many general areas in which an academic librarian operates, including administration/management, reference, cataloging, circulation, ordering, training/instruction, and organizational tasks, a large number of the responses described technical activities often performed by student workers or paraprofessionals. There were also a number of disturbing responses, including "plays computer games," "sits around," and "cleans." Reference duties were most frequently mentioned but only briefly described (e.g., "helps people"), followed by circulation-related activities, which were clearly seen as technical (e.g., "checks out books"), and cataloging/organizational tasks, which were vague (e.g., "organize material"). Language used in describing duties was simple and often seemed borrowed from retail business, including "oversee inventory," "stock books," and "log info into computer." Technology was mentioned in some descriptions of duties but not as frequently as when students were asked to describe library classes or skills librarians have.

Hernon and Pastine's respondents defined librarians' job duties in terms of the reference function. Only 3.6% of their responses suggested cataloging and organizational functions and only 2.8% an acquisitions role, which was far less than the responses to this study.[20] Their respondents referred to librarians as being "trained" and "skilled" rather than "educated" or "professional," which reflects the findings of this study as well.

Perceived duties of reference librarians in Hernon and Pastine's study emphasized their role in finding information and leading people to knowledge rather than imparting it.[21] Only 5% indicated a collection development role, and none suggested instructional/teaching functions. In our survey, instructional/teaching functions were described less frequently than other duties of academic librarians but at least 9 of 45 respondents described teaching or training in some way. Other assorted duties described by Hernon and Pastine's respondents were similar to those found in this study including managing the library, and classifying and shelving books.[22]

What Is the Student's Perception of Academic Librarians' Attitude Toward Their Jobs and Toward Students?

Students were asked to rank a list of reasons academic librarians chose their profession (Table 1); the top response was "they like books," followed by "they want to help people," and the last response was "it's an easy job." A majority (75%) of respondents agreed with the statement that librarians like helping students, but they didn't think

TABLE 1. Reasons Academic Librarians Chose Their Profession, as Ranked by Students

1. They like books.
2. They want to help people.
3. They like working with information.
4. They like working with technology.
5. They want to do library research.
6. They want to work in the university library environment (scholarly, quiet, etc.).
7. Attractive wages and benefits.
8. The prestige accompanying the job.
9. It's an easy job.

librarians like helping students with projects that are due tomorrow (63%).

Most respondents agreed that librarians respect students' intelligence (68%) and that librarians help students learn to do things themselves (77%). In a departure from previous studies, only 6 of 48 students agreed with the statement that librarians think people who don't know the basics about the library are stupid, which indicates that this is less of a reason for not asking questions. Although in previous studies students felt librarians were too busy to help them, in this survey only 6 of 48 respondents strongly agreed or agreed that librarians are too busy to help students.[23]

Respondents were less confident that librarians understand students' time pressures and that they treated each student like an individual; more than 50% of respondents either answered "neither agree nor disagree" or expressed disagreement to these questions.

Respondents seemed to have no idea if librarians are willing to change their services to meet patrons' needs; the "neither agree nor disagree" option was the most popular response, with almost equal percentages agreeing or disagreeing.

Hernon and Pastine focused on the interpersonal relations between librarians and students rather than students' perceptions of librarian attitudes toward students, and so they had no comparable data for this portion.

DISCUSSION

The results of this survey can be summarized as follows:

- Students know librarians are there to help them but often consider librarians' knowledge as limited to familiarity with the physical library.
- Students often described library school classes and librarian expertise in professional terms and correctly identified librarians at SIUC as faculty, but their descriptions of librarians' job duties included many clerical tasks.
- Even though students may think librarians are faculty, they are not aware of librarians' educational background and the professional character of a librarian's job.
- Students are aware of the increase of technology in libraries and of librarians' positive role in assisting users with technology.

- Students have a generally positive impression of librarians' attitudes toward them but aren't sure librarians are as willing to change services or to help during "crunch time."

Various suggestions have been made regarding the origin of perceptions of librarians, including the title "librarian," which may bring up images from movies, past experiences, or characters in stories, and the libraries in which they work, which vary from untouchable marble edifices to cozy, carpeted, quiet places.[24] Strategies for creating correct perceptions of librarians have also been discussed: some suggest quality work will in itself create a positive image; Blackwelder says patrons will begin seeing librarians as "key components of the information age" when librarians see themselves as such.[25] Schuman suggests some image problems stem from too much focus on the library as a place and less about the expertise of the people inside it.[26] She considers the turn of the century as a critical time when librarians can publicize their potential, particularly as libraries increase electronic services. Schuman values the existing public service and community relations programs, such as ALA's National Library Week program, but she also encourages librarians to do more, both as a group and in individual practice.[27]

Other professions often invest in advertising campaigns to boost their images; the American Academy of Family Physicians and the American Board of Family Practice spent $5.1 million on an image-building program.[28] In 1997, the American Bar Association hired a $170,000-a-year public relations expert to give lawyers an image makeover.[29] Such campaigns may be too expensive for libraries and professional organizations who are more interested in spending money on research and service that more directly connects users with information. Also, the diversity of libraries, even among academic libraries, may impair the usefulness of large campaigns. Perhaps it is better to incorporate public relations informally, by taking more care with our practice.

One direct way librarians can change college and university students' perceptions is to include information about their own education, skills, jobs, and personalities in library instruction classes. As some academic librarians reach out to high schools, opportunities expand for introducing students to today's world of librarianship before they even reach college.[30] A topic of further study in this area might be to interview students and attempt to determine how much the perception of librarians is based on experience with past librarians.

Another idea for library instruction classes is to design curriculum to indirectly address perceptions; for example, comparing what students tend to do without instruction from a librarian to what librarians have been educated to do. In a class about online databases, the teacher could first demonstrate the ineffectiveness of using one-word search queries in online databases, a common student strategy, then demonstrate use of Boolean or field searching, at which librarians are the experts. It should be emphasized that, although in class students will be learning some techniques, librarians' daily practice with the databases makes it worth a few minutes to ask them for help with tough problems.

Outside of a formal class setting, university libraries and librarians will have different misconceptions to deal with depending on the library and college or university environment. The librarians who appear too busy to help may wish to post cheerful "Ask Me Anyway!" signs. Librarians who are concerned about their professional image may wish to dress above their university standards, post degrees in a visible location, or add degree letters to nametags and nameplates. Libraries that use nametags may wish to add symbols indicating years of service to provide students with a reason for variance in expertise. Libraries that refer reference questions to subject specialists could qualify referrals, not only giving the name of a subject specialist but also adding information about his/her degrees or years of experience with the area. Technical services librarians who wish to inform others of their skills may wish to teach part or all of a library instruction class, or at least work with whoever teaches the class to develop curriculum that illustrates their work accurately.

This survey asked if knowing more about a librarian's education, skills, job, and personality would help students decide whether or not to ask librarians for help. Responses to this question were split in about equal thirds between agreement, disagreement, and neither, indicating that as a group, they just didn't know if it would help. In future library instruction classes taught by this instructor, a small class module regarding just this topic will be tested and evaluated.

Students' perceptions of librarians affect their decisions to ask for help, the amount of time they are willing to listen to a reference librarian, and their resulting success in using the library. Nationwide efforts cannot be tailored to address the diversity among academic libraries. Individual academic libraries will need to explore their own alternatives if they wish to change their students' perceptions.

REFERENCES

1. Pauline Wilson, *Stereotype and Status: Librarians in the United States* (Westport, CT: Greenwood Press, 1982).

2. Mary Jo Lynch, "1985 ALA Member Opinion Survey," *American Libraries* 17 (May 1986): 364-5.

3. Patricia G. Schuman, "The Image of Librarians: Substance or Shadow?" *Journal of Academic Librarianship* 16 (May 1990): 86-89.

4. The Center for Applications of Psychological Type conducted the MBTI in the 1970s and 1980s and assigned librarians the type ISFJ (Introverted/Sensing/Feeling/Judging), while the 1992 ACRL survey found that the two most frequent types were ISTJ (Introverted/Sensing/Thinking/Judging) and INTJ (Introverted/Intuitive/Thinking/Judging). Mary Jane Scherdin and Anne K. Beaubien, "Shattering Our Stereotype: Librarians' New Image," *Library Journal* 120 (July 1995): 35-8.

5. Julie M. Still, "The Role and Image of the Library and Librarians in Discipline-Specific Pedagogical Journals," *The Journal of Academic Librarianship* 24 (May 1998): 225-31.

6. Gordon Flagg, "Librarians Share Image Issues with the Popular Culture Association," *American Libraries* 30 (May 1999): 28-9.

7. Numerous columns under the titles "AL Aside–Image" and "Image: How They're Seeing Us" in *American Libraries*. Will Manley, "Our Image, as Images Go," *American Libraries* 27 (May 1996): 136. Murray S. Martin, "Who are We? Professional Image of Librarians," *Technicalities* 18 (Mar. 1998): 4-5.

8. Peter Hernon and Maureen Pastine, "Student Perceptions of Academic Librarians," *College and Research Libraries* 38 (Mar. 1977): 129-139.

9. Philip J. Egan, "Bridging the Gap Between the Student and the Library," *College Teaching* 41 (Spring 1992): 67-70. Anne Fliotsos, "Anxiety Layering: The Effects of Library and Computer Anxiety on CD-ROM Use," *The Southeastern Library*, 42 (Summer 1992): 47-49. Qun Jiao, Anthony Onwuegbuzie, and Arthur A. Lichtenstein, "Library Anxiety: Characteristics of At-Risk College Students," *Library and Information Science Research*, 18 (Spring 1996): 151-163. Qun G. Jiao and Anthony J. Onwuegbuzie, "Identifying Library Anxiety Through Students' Learning Modality Preferences," *Library Quarterly* 69 (Apr. 1999): 202-16. Carol C. Kuhlthau, "Developing a Model of the Library Search Process: Cognitive and Affective Aspects," *RQ* 28 (Winter 1998): 232-242. ———, "Inside the Search Process: Information Seeking from the User's Perspective," *Journal of the American Society for Information Science* 42 (June 1991): 361-371. Terrence F. Mech and Charles I. Brooks, "Library Anxiety Among College Students: An Exploratory Study," Paper presented at the 7th National Conference of the Association for College and Research Libraries, Pittsburgh, PA, 30 March-2 April 1995. Constance A. Mellon, "Library Anxiety: A Grounded Theory and Its Development," *College and Research Libraries* 47 (Mar. 1986): 160-155. ———, "Attitudes: the Forgotten Dimension in Library Instruction," *Library Journal*, 113 (1 Sep. 1988): 137-9. Lynn Westbrook and Sharon DeDecker, "Supporting User Needs and Skills to Minimize Library Anxiety: Considerations for Academic Libraries," *The Reference Librarian* 40 (1993): 43-51. (The former article lists suggestions for improvement of the relationship).

10. Mary Jane Swope and Jeffrey Katzer, "Why Don't They Ask Questions?" *RQ* (Winter 1972): 161-5. Desmond B. Hatchard and Phyllis Toy, "The Psychological Barriers Between Library Users and Library Staff," *Australian Academic and Research Libraries* (June 1986): 63-9. Virginia Boucher, "Nonverbal Communication and the Library Reference Interview," *RQ* (Fall 1976): 27-31. Ralph Gers and Lillie Seward, "Improving Reference Performance: Results of a Statewide Study," *Library Journal* (1 Nov. 1985): 32-5.

11. Mellon, "Library Anxiety," 160.

12. Swope and Katzer, "Why Don't They Ask Questions?" 161-5.

13. Jiao, Onwuegbuzie, and Lichtenstein, "Library Anxiety," 151-163.

14. Renee Rude and Robert Hauptman, "To Serve the Unserved: Social Responsibility in the Academy," *Journal of Academic Librarianship*, 15 (Jan. 1990): 364-5.

15. Hernon and Pastine, "Student Perceptions," 131.

16. Ibid., 133.

17. Ibid., 136.

18. Ibid., 133.

19. Ibid.

20. Ibid., 132.

21. Ibid.

22. Ibid., 133.

23. Ibid., 134.

24. Mark Field, "It's Not Our Name That's the Problem," *Library Association Record* 101 (Aug. 1999): 449. Mary B. Blackwelder, "The Image of Health Sciences Librarians: How We See Ourselves and How Patrons See Us," *Bulletin of the Medical Library Association*. 84 (July 1996): 345.

25. Blackwelder, 346.

26. Schuman, 88.

27. Ibid.

28. Special Libraries Association, *Report on the Enhancement of the Image of the Librarian/Information Profession*, (Washington, D.C.: Special Libraries Association, 1991).

29. Manley, "Our Image, as Images Go," *American Libraries* 27 (May 1996): 136.

30. Margot Sutton, "Job Shadow Day 2000: Recruiting to the Profession," *College and Research Libraries News* 61 (Apr 2000): 295-6, 311.

APPENDIX A. Survey

Objective: To discover the perceptions of SIUC undergraduate students regarding librarians.
Terms which may require definition: librarian: Academic librarian at a university similar to SIUC
Specific Objectives:

1. Do students know which workers in their library are librarians?
2. What do students think librarians do?
3. What kind of knowledge, skills, and expertise do students think librarians have?
4. What level of education do students think librarians have?
5. Do students perceive librarians as valuable to the University?
6. Do students perceive librarians as valuable to their own education?
7. What do students perceive is the librarian's role in the University?
8. What do students perceive is the librarian's role in their own education?
9. What is the student's perception of the librarian's attitude toward students?
10. What are the reasons students don't ask librarians questions?
11. Do students who consulted librarians in K-12 schooling feel more confident about consulting University librarians?
12. Is there a correlation between gender and these answers?
13. Is there a correlation between grade level and these answers?
14. Do students who have consulted librarians more often have different perceptions of librarians than students who do not consult librarians? How do they differ?

What do you think about librarians?

Note: for the purposes of this survey, the phrase "academic librarians" will refer to librarians who work in libraries at universities like SIUC.

You and your experience with librarians:

1. I am a (circle one): Freshman   Sophomore   Junior   Senior
   Other: _____

2. I am a (circle one):   Male   Female

3. How often have you consulted librarians in a public library?

	Never	Less than once per year	1-5 times per year	Once a month	More than once a month
In grade school and junior high school (K-8)?					
In High School (9-12)?					

4. How often did you consult **your school's** librarian?

    ___ My grade school didn't have a librarian (check if this applies)
    ___ My junior high school didn't have a librarian (check if this applies)
    ___ My high school didn't have a librarian (check if this applies)

	Never	Less than once per year	1-5 times per year	Once a month	More than once a month
In grade school and junior high school (K-8)?					
In High School (9-12)?					

5. Do you feel that librarians helped you succeed **in grade and junior high school** education?
__ Yes __ No

6. Do you feel that librarians helped you succeed **in high school** education?
__ Yes __ No

7. How often have you consulted an **academic librarian** during your college years?

Never	Less than once per year	1-5 times per year	Once a month	More than once a month

8. Do you feel that academic librarians have helped you succeed in your college education?
__ Yes __ No

The Job:

9. Please rank the following reasons librarians chose to become librarians 1-9, where 1 is the top reason that librarians want to be librarians.

__ they want to work in the university library environment (scholarly, quiet, etc.)
__ they like books
__ attractive wages and benefits
__ they want to do library research
__ the prestige accompanying the job
__ they want to help people
__ they like working with information
__ they like working with technology
__ it's an easy job

Other reasons you'd like to add: _____

10. In Morris Library, can you tell which library workers are librarians?
__ Yes __ No

11. In Morris Library, do you ever specifically ask to speak to a librarian?
__ Yes __ No

12. What do academic librarians do all day? Write at least five different job duties you think an academic librarian performs regularly:
1.
2.
3.
4.
5.

APPENDIX A (continued)

13. Do you think academic librarians are considered faculty at this University?
    __ Yes __ No

14. Do you think academic librarians are considered faculty at every University?
    __ Yes __ No

15. Do you think academic librarians are required to do research like faculty members?
    __ Yes __ No

16. How much do you think an entry-level academic librarian makes per year?
    __ less than $15,000
    __ $15,000
    __ $20,000
    __ $25,000
    __ $30,000
    __ $35,000
    __ $40,000
    __ $50,000
    __ more than $50,000

17. What skills do librarians have that are valuable to you?
    1.
    2.
    3.
    4.
    5.

18. Do you think librarians are useful to the University in ways that don't directly relate to students?
    __ Yes __ No

    If so, what skills do librarians have that are valuable to the University?
    1.
    2.
    3.
    4.
    5.

19. Why **don't** you like to ask librarians questions?
    1.
    2.
    3.
    4.
    5.

20. Why **do** you like to ask librarians questions?
    1.
    2.
    3.
    4.
    5.

Education:

21. What educational qualifications do you think an entry level academic librarian must have? (**check all that apply**)
___ high school degree
___ Some college classes
___ Bachelor's degree
___ Master's degree
___ more than one Master's degree
___ Doctoral degree
___ Multiple Doctoral degrees

22. What do you think academic librarians learn in their library classes? Please write at least five topics you think are covered in library school classes:
1.
2.
3.
4.
5.

General Opinions:

23. Please read the following statements carefully and indicate your level of agreement, where 1 = strongly agree, 5 = strongly disagree

Remember, "Librarians" means academic librarians at a university like SIUC.

	Strongly Agree	Agree	Neither Agree nor Disagree	Disagree	Strongly Disagree
Librarians like helping students	1	2	3	4	5
Librarians are slow	1	2	3	4	5
Librarians like helping students with projects that are due tomorrow	1	2	3	4	5
Librarians respect students' intelligence	1	2	3	4	5
Librarians help students learn to do things themselves	1	2	3	4	5
Librarians think people who don't know the basics about the library are stupid	1	2	3	4	5
Librarians are too busy to help students	1	2	3	4	5
It is faster for me to figure out a tough question myself rather than ask a librarian	1	2	3	4	5
Librarians understand students' time pressures	1	2	3	4	5
Librarians are easy to talk to	1	2	3	4	5

APPENDIX A (continued)

	Strongly Agree	Agree	Neither Agree nor Disagree	Disagree	Strongly Disagree
Librarians are willing to change their services to meet patrons' needs	1	2	3	4	5
Librarians use words that I don't understand	1	2	3	4	5
Librarians know what they're doing	1	2	3	4	5
Librarians have difficult jobs	1	2	3	4	5
Librarians treat each student like an individual	1	2	3	4	5
Helping students is a librarian's #1 priority	1	2	3	4	5
Librarians have knowledge that is practical to me	1	2	3	4	5
Librarians are friendly and pleasant	1	2	3	4	5
Librarians are experts with technology	1	2	3	4	5
I would rather ask a female librarian for help (rather than a male librarian)	1	2	3	4	5
Librarians help me search the Internet more effectively	1	2	3	4	5
Knowing more about a librarian's education, skills, job, and personality help me decide whether or not to ask them for help	1	2	3	4	5
There are more female librarians than male librarians	1	2	3	4	5
I would be more willing to approach a librarian of my own race or ethnicity	1	2	3	4	5
There is enough diversity (race, ethnicity, age, gender, etc.) among librarians	1	2	3	4	5
It is important to employ librarians of diverse ages, races, and gender	1	2	3	4	5

Any additional comments?

THANK YOU for completing this survey!

FUTURE TRENDS

The Enhanced and Changing Role of the Specialist Librarian: Survey of Education Librarians

Johnnieque B. (Johnnie) Love

SUMMARY. Much like the role of other academic librarians, the education librarian's responsibilities are in a constant state of transition. Major factors contributing to these changes are demands being placed on teacher training programs in colleges of education, demands placed on teachers and administrators in the nation's schools, demographic shifts, globalization, declining accessibility of resources along with the digital divide, and, most of all, greater demands for accountability of student achievement at all levels of education.

The work of the education librarian has become more integrated in the creation and access of knowledge both in the library profession, and education itself. Education librarians not only have close ties to school cur-

Johnnieque B. (Johnnie) Love is Coordinator of Personnel Programs, Personnel & Budget Department, Planning & Administrative Services Division, University of Maryland Libraries, College Park, MD 20742 (E-mail: jl345@umail.umd.edu).

[Haworth co-indexing entry note]: "The Enhanced and Changing Role of the Specialist Librarian: Survey of Education Librarians." Love, Johnnieque B. Co-published simultaneously in *The Reference Librarian* (The Haworth Information Press, an imprint of The Haworth Press, Inc.) No. 78, 2002, pp. 149-165; and: *The Image and Role of the Librarian* (ed: Wendi Arant, and Candace R. Benefiel) The Haworth Information Press, an imprint of The Haworth Press, Inc., 2002, pp. 149-165. Single or multiple copies of this article are available for a fee from The Haworth Document Delivery Service [1-800-HAWORTH, 9:00 a.m. - 5:00 p.m. (EST). E-mail address: docdelivery@haworthpress.com].

http://www.haworthpress.com/store/product.asp?sku=J120
10.1300/J120v37n78_10

riculum being taught but also with the preparation of preservice teachers, students enrolled in advanced graduate studies, and the education researcher. This article will review the literature on the role of the education subject specialist in librarianship, and how that role has been changed due to a variety of reasons. Findings will be discussed from an informal survey on how education librarians perceive their roles in their institutions. *[Article copies available for a fee from The Haworth Document Delivery Service: 1-800-HAWORTH. E-mail address: <docdelivery@haworthpress. com> Website: <http://www.HaworthPress.com> © 2002 by The Haworth Press, Inc. All rights reserved.]*

KEYWORDS. Library roles, education, education research, academic library specialization, education librarians and collaborative learning, curriculum development, librarian-teacher cooperation

INTRODUCTION

Over the past decade, numerous changes have affected the role of the academic librarian. These changes have subsequently affected all subject specialists and their roles in the grand scheme of the university and academic mission. The enhanced and changing role of the education librarian, like all academic librarians, has been transformed by technology, changes in electronic information formats, and the impact of technology on all levels of our society. Much like the role of the classroom teacher, and academic faculty, the role and responsibilities of the education librarian are in continuous motion and therefore transition.

Rapple (1997) states the new technology in hardware, software, and infrastructure of the institution make up only part of the change. He adds that an even greater change has occurred within the library culture itself. Our daily routine has changed as to how we perform our duties and responsibilities. We have become totally dependent on technology for all library technical work because it brings consistency and uniformity in how we provide our services (1997, p. 114). In other words, the reality of change in the academic library must be recognized, for it redefines how the education librarian provides services to meet users, needs.

First, the role and work of the education librarian is similar to that of the academic librarian due to common environment. The education librarian, as with librarians in other fields with background, experience and/or advanced degrees in a specific discipline, has become a research consultant for the clientele they serve. What has been found is that much of the research on the academic librarian's role and work may be adapted and applied to the work and role of the education librarian as well.

In our society the mission and purpose of education has made it necessary for the education librarian to be knowledgeable of the changes taking place within the discipline. According to Skiadas (1999), the purpose of education is still the same as it was in its initial efforts; and that is to perpetuate knowledge, and to advance and extend to future generations. He concludes, "Knowledge is closely connected to the culture from which it originates, and is transmitted through education. As a result, education has become an essential cultural institution" (1999, p. 1). We must also provide assistance to faculty for the classroom to ensure that educational outcomes are positive and productive. The enhanced role of the specialist librarian in education means that there is a greater understanding and acquisition of:

- Knowledge of the developmental process of learners.
- Knowledge of learning theory and how they relate to information skills instruction.
- Increasing knowledge of curriculum resources for K-12 grades, and use of technology in the instructional process.
- Working with preservice teachers to integrate literature with technology.
- Knowledge of how to use the Internet as an instructional tool.
- Design marketing strategies for services to users.

The specialist librarian must be proactive, using new strategies for instruction, and facilitating the process by which students become more effective learners. Ultimate responsibility is to assist the university in its role of developing students as citizens, leaders, and life-long learners. We must be visionary in preparing future educators, for their knowledge base will have a significant and direct impact on the ability, opportunity and knowledge gained by the students they will be teaching. Therefore, the education librarian is charged with informing students, faculty and future educators of the wealth, depth and variety of resources that can make their work more creative and challenging for, and with, their students.

DEFINING THE SPECIALIST LIBRARIAN'S ROLE

For the sake of discussion, and for clarification of the role of the specialist librarian's work, it is essential that we examine the term "role."

According to Webster's tenth edition, the term role means a "character assigned or assumed; a socially accepted behavior pattern usually determined by an individual's status in a particular societal position and/or community." The *International Encyclopedia* of *Social Sciences* expands upon this definition and adds that role is the process of continuous self-examination, self-definition, and self-assessment thereby incorporating behavioral changes. It is also a process of assembling and transmitting the norms of one's culture and aspiration that meet the needs of the academic community (1994, p. 1660).

The role of the specialist librarian is directly reflected and impacted by the role and mission of the academic library. Its mission in the twenty-first century is the same as it has been ever since libraries came into existence; simply stated, it is to supply students and staff with access to the information they need. Just as the academic library's mission is teaching, research and community service, the specialist librarian must integrate these tenets in all patterns of public service. Whereas, the traditional role of the specialist librarian has been to acquire new resources, process them, establish circulation procedures for those resources, and provide assistance to information seekers whether they are driven by classroom assignments or by research. Skiadas states that in order to fulfill the core mission successfully, it is necessary that emphasis be placed on new functions and skills such as defining user needs, development of new products and services, user help, information analysis, and marketing of information products to serve users (1999, p. 7). Skiadas emphasizes that in order for the academic library to ensure its continued relevance in this new century it must move from an operational mode of ownership to an access mode of operation, and from "re-active to pro-active" involvement in the academic community. Nahl (1996) agrees on these assumptions of services, but adds that we must exceed what are considered acceptable standards. In other words, our new goal for service should be in the mode of "over-delivery of our services by extending ourselves to those who need support, understanding the best practices of education theory and following them, and managing the change that we are constantly faced with" (1996, p. 3).

Education librarians are more integrated in the creation and access of knowledge than ever before in the library profession. We not only have close ties to school curriculum being taught, but also with education majors, doctoral students and the active education researcher. As specialist librarians, it is our mission to instruct students in ways that will increase their ability to utilize skills and conduct research, thereby improving their critical thinking and evaluative competencies of new information. The role of the specialist librarian will reach its height of change when the emphasis will be completely placed on developing a "critical consciousness." Shifflett (1996) quotes Louis Shor, one of the early contemporary library leaders as saying that "we need to examine how we see ourselves in relation to knowledge and power in our society, the way we act in the library and daily life, and to reproduce and transform our conditions for service."

The enhanced and changing role of the specialist librarian must become one where greater emphasis is consistently placed on "user-centeredness." Nahl (1995) describes this concept as awareness and a higher level of consciousness of "users," their resource needs, and how the academic library must manage the users' needs for information. In this paradigm the specialist librarian is driven by a moral commitment to help students be prepared to serve their future students. This concept is central to redesigning how services are to be provided. It means a shift from traditional bibliographic instruction to bibliographic instruction designed to be more interactive with an access-based approach focused on active learning and critical thinking. Bibliographic Instruction Design places an emphasis on the needs and behaviors of information seekers in complex information environments (Ibid. p. 7).

GUIDELINES DEVELOPED TO GUIDE THE WORK OF THE SPECIALIST LIBRARIAN IN EDUCATION

During the 1980s educators, school librarians and education librarians became extremely concerned about the skills students needed in order to become effective users of electronic information. The American Library Association has led the way by defining and providing direction for librarians and educators alike. In 1992, the Association for College and Research Libraries (ACRL) became visionaries in providing structure for education librarians when the Education and Behavioral Sciences Section of ACRL issued a document called the "Information Retrieval and Evaluation Skills for Education Students." The purpose of this document was to assist education librarians in working with education faculty to integrate information literacy skills training into the teacher training programs. It details the goals, objectives, and predicted outcomes of competencies in five major categories:

• Generation and communication of information and knowledge in education,

- Intellectual access,
- Bibliographic representations of information sources,
- Physical access and evaluation of information sources, and
- Collaborative roles of teachers and librarians (ACRL, 2000).

Rader's (1997) research identifies other accrediting agencies that have recognized the importance of information literacy in the curricula of colleges and universities, and the important role librarians should assume in the teaching-learning environment. Departments of education, higher education commissions, and academic governing boards have begun to take a stand in advocating the development of information literacy skills. In 1994, agencies such as the Commission on Higher Education, Middle States Association of Colleges and Schools, joined with ACRL and the National Forum on Information Literacy to develop initiatives that would provide a broad definition of literacy that included electronic information sources.

It is the responsibility of the education librarian to inform teacher education programs of the need to include strategies for information literacy in their course work and to see how strategies can be accomplished through cooperative ventures with the library staff. Research in student progress shows learning occurs more rapidly when students are actively involved, when it is collaborative, and when current information sources are utilized in the process. Collaborative efforts inherently produce critical thinking skills that promote the ability of learners to become life-long learners in their skill development. Rader emphasizes that only through the joint efforts of faculty and education librarians will students be able to develop information literacy skills that meet the demands of their course requirements (1997, p. 2).

SPECIALIST LIBRARIAN IN EDUCATION
AS LIAISON AND LEADER

The role of the specialist librarian has always been to facilitate the access of information. However, this role has experienced revitalization in the university community due to the rapid changes in information, and the need for users to know how to access information. Traditionally, reference service has focused on instruction utilizing those resources found within the four walls of the library. Today this is no longer possible. We can now say that we partner with education faculty so that they might have knowledge of information sources, and find ways to develop new pedagogical strategies. Haynes (1996) argues that librarians are far more capable than anyone else in the academic community of guiding students through a myriad of information sources because they are, by far, the most capable of helping students discover relationships. Our basic and primary role is to assist students in finding the information they need regardless of the capability of the user, age, socio-economic background and access to information. In addition to the variety of instructional tasks, the key responsibility of the education librarian is to serve as liaison to the education faculty. In this capacity, the education librarian provides leadership and advocacy in collection management as well as fiscal direction for acquisition of resources.

If the library professional is to survive in this age of responsibilities being dictated by technology and diminished fiscal resources, we must find strategies for developing collaborative opportunities with faculty in order to meet educational goals of the university. Jeffery's (1998) research aligns with Haynes. He argues that it is no longer feasible for library professionals to operate in isolation, and concludes that it should become a priority for librarians to become emerged in collaborative efforts that integrate highly specialized information. In addition, he adds:

> We must be willing to integrate methodology, diplomacy and broad content knowledge necessary to orchestrate collaborative projects. We must not only participate in cooperative ventures within our library organizations, but develop a professional ethic of leadership through the collaborative process. (1998, p. 28)

Smith (1995) concurs with both Rapple and Haynes on the concept of librarians as leaders and advocates, but also adds that the specialist librarian can no longer "side-step" technology usage. They must be able to move toward, adapt, assess, embrace and grow with the powerful uses of technology. In doing so, they will find themselves serving in a variety of roles; i.e., counselor, facilitator, and collaborator rather than just being an information intermediary.

THE IMPACT OF THE EDUCATION LIBRARIAN ON PRESERVICE AND FUTURE TEACHERS

According to Coaldrake and Stedman, 1998, p. 42, . . . the best education a person could receive would be one where they learned how to learn, . . . and this is far more important than learning particular facts or techniques. Universities which provide a stimulating, broad and challenging education, for young people in particular, should be highly valued. (Skiadas, 1999)

This statement by Coaldrake and Stedman creates an imperative for new directions in how preservice teachers are being prepared to meet the challenge of their responsibilities in the nation's classrooms. Action research is one of the new concepts of instruction that is making an important change in education and how teachers and administrators view their work. It is systemic inquiry conducted by teacher researchers and other stakeholders in the teaching/learning environment. The concept has brought a change to professional attitudes, one that positions teachers and administrators as learners rather than experts.

Mills (2000) argues that action research fosters a democratic approach to decision-making while it empowers individual teachers through participation in collaborative, socially responsive research activity. According to Mills, "Action research will rejuvenate the teaching of curriculum development, authentic assessment strategies, classroom management, teaching strategies, and ultimately, caring for children" (2000, p. 6).

An example of action research is the implementation of "Project Inquiry," in the College of Education at Texas A&M University. The program is in its pilot stages, serving 10 students in 2000, and will expand to work with thirty-four students, and a host of mentoring teachers in the classrooms of local school districts in the 2001-2002 academic year. Preservice teachers will incorporate information literacy competencies with pedagogical theory and research to do in-depth study of the classroom field experience. Incorporating action research will infuse the teacher education program with a focus of research opportunities in the classroom, and knowledge of research and professional development.

RESEARCH APPLICABLE
TO THE EDUCATION LIBRARIAN'S ROLE

One of the most significant studies of the academic library and role of the academic librarian in the new millennium is a Delphi study published by Feret and Marcinek of Poland (1999). The study examines how information experts envision the academic library by the year 2005. Four key issues served as the focus: impact factors, library activities, skill sets needed by librarians, and problems encountered with new technologies and electronic media. Researchers were able to identify several conclusions about the probable state of academic libraries in 2005.

Their first conclusion drawn was that respondents felt overall financial policies have the most impact on all library activities. But the lack of funding will not be a hindrance to providing desired activities and services. The main impact on changing patterns of library services will be derived from factors other than funding levels. This is not a new status for libraries. As an institution, we have never really had great sums of funds to provide the much-needed services for our users and communities.

The second conclusion drawn from the study was that the library will not only serve but will also be involved in teaching and education to an even greater degree than it is now. Intensive and extensive training for users in techniques of data retrieval, involvement in distance learning, and patterns of teaching and learning techniques will be necessary. Due to the complexity of future retrieval tools, the users will become dependent upon guidance in the use of these resources. Training users will be one of the most important services of the user-oriented library. The librarian will have to be equipped with advanced-level technology skills. The study has estimated that over fifty percent of library activities will be related to information management and training. The area of greatest development will be document delivery services.

A third conclusion was that academic library staff should become comfortable in providing various kinds of services. "The academic librarian of the twenty-first century must be a researcher, counselor, planner, manager, assessor, team member, problem-solver and computer repairman" (1999, p. 9). This perception of the academic librarian's role appears to be a common one in the literature. The author goes on to say that one of the most valuable attributes of the academic librarian in 2005 will be as it is now–"to have a good sense of humor." Future library staff will have to keep up with the pace of change–continual hands-on training, professional courses, seminars and workshops will all be incorporated. Seeing as how a significant number of these conclusions are already true today, librarians will have to be prepared for life-long learning experiences at all times.

James Neal's (1996) article entitled "Academic Libraries: 2000 and Beyond," expresses similar comments and perceptions as stated in the Delphi Study. However, Neal predicts that the academic library funding will remain stable while the need for services will increase. He estimates the greatest growth will be in collection and information access programs. Neal addresses one critical issue that is not mentioned in the other research: academic libraries have not responded effectively to demographic, cultural, racial and ethnic shifts. This issue has become a global issue.

Neal points out that academic libraries will, collectively, enter the new millennium without recognizing the demographic trends; nor will they have a well-coordinated plan for the role and contributions the academic library can make to a multicultural society. In comparison, public libraries are fulfilling their mission of becoming a force for community building (1996, p. 2).

Byron's (1995) study of faculty satisfaction was based on responses provided by the College of Arts and Sciences faculty at the University of North Texas and their perceptions of the library's value to teaching and research, and was an attempt to learn what encourages faculty to make greater use of the library. The following common themes have emerged. Faculty felt the need for greater access to electronic journals, coupled with the library's role to provide assistance to all students. The consensus from the focus groups revealed a positive perception of the library staff. Faculty acknowledged the importance and critical need for library instruction. They also knew they needed assistance from experts on teaching information literacy and critical thinking skills for conducting research. Faculty also felt the need to strengthen the role of the library liaison so that they could be more informed on how to access electronic resources.

INFORMAL SURVEY
OF SELECTED EDUCATION LIBRARIANS' PERCEPTIONS
OF THEIR ROLE

The work of the education subject specialist has become so highly specialized that it is difficult to keep up with all that is taking place in this area of librarianship as well as in the discipline of education. With the changes in areas of technology, the discipline of education itself, economics, collection development, and accessing information in the academic library, it becomes necessary to continuously address multiple issues simultaneously.

Several objectives were identified for the purpose of this survey. First, to determine the perceptions of the education librarian's role and work, and to identify what makes the services they provide distinctively unique within their institution. Second, the author wanted to obtain perceptions of the education librarian's role in their academic environment. The third objective was to determine if the education librarians' workload had increased due to technology. The fourth objective was to examine the extent to which education was emphasized in academic libraries, and last, to identify the level of resources available to students for teacher preparation. The author also wanted to determine if the existing roles of the selected education librarians were similar to those written about in the literature.

Thirty surveys were sent out to a selected group of education librarians. Fifty percent of the surveys were returned. The selected education librarians were from a variety of academic institutions with different focuses for education within the libraries. One person returning the survey stated that she was not a librarian but was education faculty who worked closely with the library and taught children's literature courses in the library. Five of the respondents had multiple roles within their libraries. Eleven of the respondents had specific education roles but economics play a critical role in the development of their collections. The informal survey was made up of six questions. Findings from the six questions follow.

Informal Survey Questions

1. There are various specialties within the area of education librarianship. What do you consider your academic library's emphasis for education that makes your role as education librarian unique? (Example: Do you have a resource center for education majors or do you provide textbook and juvenile literature resources?)

In question 1, eleven out of the fifteen returning surveys stated that their library collections included state-adopted textbook resources. Six of the education librarians stated that their libraries had a curriculum and/or materials resource center to provide extra resources for preservice teachers. One respondent stated that the resources center resembled a model public school library, providing resources that support the teacher education program, because the program was well supported on their campus. Three other education librarians stated that they provide reference services, bibliographic instruction, and one-on-one consulting reference service.

The literature collections in these institutions varied greatly. Seven of the education librarians said their libraries provided children's and young adult literature resources, while one librarian revealed that they only provided Newbery and Caldecott titles in their collection due to a small budget.

Few of the selected respondents were full time education librarians. Five had other responsibilities in their libraries. One librarian stated that she worked in a two-person operation, with both persons being overworked; therefore she did not have time to provide services that were specifically directed to education majors.

2. As an education librarian, what do you see as essential leadership qualities for public service and for creating greater visibility for your role as education librarian?

Education librarians responding to this question agreed on the many different aspects of public service work. Respondents used such attributes as assertive, approachable, available, organized, and having excellent teaching skills to describe the essential qualities that are needed by today's education librarians if they plan to create greater visibility for their public service efforts.

Just as in the review of the literature, many of the respondents agreed on the concept that education librarians must be aggressive and proactive in marketing their services, and in their effort to collaborate with faculty. Since electronic resources and technology are central to the library's services, it is up to education librarians to make sure faculty members are well informed about how to use these new resources as well as when new resources are acquired. In other words, we must dedicate ourselves to promoting technology resources because they provide greater access to an array of information. This concept is also presented in the literature. It also states that we should oversell our services.

Respondents also stated the importance of providing all forms of reference service, from group and/or class instruction to reference work by appointment. Two of the respondents felt that they have increased their visibility by teaching and serving as adjunct faculty. Responses to this question also made it clear that education librarians must be creative with limited fiscal resources in order to enhance and develop collections. Finally, it was a consensus by all education librarians who responded that one must be knowledgeable and have a healthy respect for the discipline of education, and understand the interdisciplinary nature of its content.

3. What do you see as the major challenges to providing the best possible services to your library users?

The major challenges in the academic library have been in the area of access and electronic resources. Overwhelming concern was expressed by the education librarians who responded about their need to feel competent in the use of electronic resources before teaching them to students. Access to electronic resources seems to be the driving force behind providing the best possible services to library users. Librarians expressed that since a large number of students are competent in the use of technology, they want to be able to have remote access to resources. The demand is there for education librarians to stay current and ahead of their users, and also to work with faculty, keeping them abreast of not only electronic resources, but also changing services such as electronic reserves and document delivery. Education librarians in small institutions felt that technology has broadened the scope of resources for them but has stretched their budgets and the librarians' learning curve beyond the breaking point. A major concern expressed was time allocated for training so that librarians could feel competent in providing instruction on electronic resources.

4. What are the demands and/or requirements being placed on education majors and/or researchers that impact your professional responsibilities?

The answers to this question varied a great deal. While some mentioned they had not seen any changes in twenty years, others were able to be very specific about accountability, technology and multiculturalism. Several of the respondents felt that education majors are under pressure to pass state mandated exams before teaching. Many of the librarians expressed that they spend a significant amount of time assisting students in the preparation for these exams. In addition to the exams, education majors are being required to be knowledgeable about technology and how to use it effectively in the classroom. Some of the respondents stated that their institutions have required courses that address each of the issues mentioned above.

Our changing demographics present education majors with the challenge of becoming knowledgeable about other cultures. Education courses of study are requiring students to become informed about multiculturalism, other ethnic groups and their cultures within their respective communities. In addition, due to lack of other exposure, students need to know more about the literature and customs of cultures different from their own. As teachers, they will need to show compassion to learners. In order to do so they will need to know more about the children they will serve. What the author found difficult to believe was that two respondents expressed that they were not aware of any changes or demands being placed on students by the education requirements.

5. How would you describe the faculty involvement in your collection development of education resources?

The answers to this question range from minimal involvement of faculty to extensive in the selection of resources for the curriculum or education resources for the general collection. One respondent felt that when there is an active faculty member that pushes the involvement of their colleagues, the input is greater. Several of the respondents who mentioned faculty involvement in the collection development process were positive about the interaction and felt that faculty knew the collection better when they gave input. Various selection methods for collection development were discussed. Blackwell's listing of approvals and *Choice* reviews were mentioned as selection tools.

6. As education librarian and/or liaison how do you view your role in regards to instruction? What is the frequency of your instructional efforts?

The majority of the education librarians stated that instructional sessions are provided upon request. Most stated that they provide instructional sessions; some had heavier class loads than others. Instructional sessions were being provided for upper level undergraduate courses and graduate level courses. Usually the heaviest load of classes falls at the beginning of each semester.

Comments provided in the informal survey were closely in line with topics presented in the literature and research. For that reason we can draw conclusions that education librarians are experiencing the stress of technology, along with economic restraints that prevent adequate collection development and an abundance of requests for instructional needs. The librarians did express concerns about the need to be trained in the use of electronic resources, but their frustration was that there was not adequate time for them to be trained before having to demonstrate to students how to use electronic resources. Some mentioned their collaborative work with faculty; others felt that faculty were not knowledgeable on the use of electronic resources themselves and did not feel comfortable in demonstrating these resources to their students. How do we address these issues? And how do we bring comfort to those who are worn and frazzled with overload? Each individual academic library has an obligation to its library staff and user community. Library administration has the responsibility to answer these questions, and establish priorities to be totally involved and committed to the educational mission of their institution.

CONCLUSION

The education librarian is viewed as a member of the scholarly community who provides expertise and support to the training of preservice teachers and other education professionals. He or she is charged with the responsibility of collaborating with faculty and supporting the teaching goals of all curriculum taught in the education department and/or college of education. As education specialist in the academic library, we should have a vision and moral commitment to play a major role in improving the learning opportunities for all students and users. We have the responsibility of teaching users the importance of critical thinking and determining the credibility of sources.

If ever there was a time and need for collaboration and consortium building, the time is now. All major factors contributing to the changes and demands being placed on teacher training programs in our colleges of education, demands placed on teachers and administrators in our nation's schools, demographic shifts, globalization, declining accessibility of resources along with the digital divide, and, most of all, greater demands for accountability of student achievement at all levels of education need to be addressed as we make changes brought on by our use of technology.

Communication must become stronger and more effective, and partnerships must be established between faculty and librarians in order to meet institutional educational goals for every student who enters the doors of the academy. This study reinforces the assumption that the education librarian's workload is heavily impacted by a number of variables. Personally and professionally, the education librarian should always be in the process of continuous self-examination, self-definition, and self-assessment because change brought on by technology and other factors will dictate the direction and format for how services should be provided.

BIBLIOGRAPHY

Bruce, N.J. (1998, 25 May). The role of the librarian in the electronic library. Philadelphia: Medical Library Association Conference: Veterinary Medical Libraries Section.

Burkhardt, R.R. (1999). A role transformed: Technology's challenge for job responsibilities of the reference librarian. *Advances in Library Administration and Organization*. JAI Press Inc. (14), 125-190.

Butcher, K. (1999, September). Reflections on academic librarianship. *Journal of Academic Librarianship*. 25 (5), 350-53.

Byron, S. (1997, March). Faculty perceptions of library support for teaching and research: A focus group study with selected faculty from the College of Arts and Sciences. *U. S. Texas*. 1997 03-31.

Butcher, K. (1999, September). Reflections on academic librarianship. *Journal of Academic Librarianship*. 25 (5), 350-53.

Ensor, P. (1997, April). Credibility and accuracy on the web: The Librarians' role. *Technicalities*. 17 (4), 2-4.

Feret, B. J. and M. Marcinek (1999, May). The future of the academic library and the academic librarian–A Delphi Study. Poland 1999. 05-00.

Gage, M. (2000). Standards fulfillment and competencies. Association of College and Research Libraries. Chicago: American Library Association. http://www.ala.org/acrl/ilcomstan.html.

Grealy, S.D. (1997). Leveraging the wave: The role of today's academic reference Librarian. *The Reference Librarian*. The Haworth Press, Inc., 59, 93-102.

Hawkins, B.L and P. Battin (1997, Spring). The changing role of the information resources professional: A dialogue. *Cause/Effect*. 20 (1), 22-30.

Haycock, K. (2000, April). Quality of profssional education. *Teacher Librarian*. 27 (4). CLIS Technical Report. No. 99-10.

Haynes, E.B. (1996). Library faculty partnerships in instruction. *Advances in Librarianship*. 20, 191-213.

Howze, P.C. and F.E. Unaeze. (1997, Spring). All in the name of service: Mediation, client self-determination, and reference practice in academic libraries. *RQ*. 36 (3), 430-437.

Jeffrey. J.R. (1998). Librarians as generalist: Redefining our role in a new paradigm. *Art Documentation*. 17 (2), 25-29.

Low, K. (1996). The Future role of Librarians: Will it change? *The Reference Librarian*. The Haworth Press, Inc., 54, 145-151.

Mills, G. (2000). *Action Research: A guide for teacher research*. Columbus, Ohio: Merrill.

Nahl, D. (1996). The user centered revolution: 1970-1995. *Encyclopedia of Microcomputers*. New York: Marcel Dekker, Inc., Vol. 19, p. 143-199.

Nahl's homepage: http://www2.hawaii.edu/~nahl/articles/user.

Neal, J.G. (1996, July). Academic libraries: 2000 and beyond. *Library Journal*. 121 (12), 74-76.

Newton-Smith, C. (1995, August). A Librarian without a library: The role of the librarian in an electronic age? Curtin University Library, pp. 1-7.

Rader, H.B. (1997). Educating students for the Information age: The role of the librarian. *RSR: Reference Service Review.* 25 (2), 47-52.

Rapple, B. A. (1997, Spring). The Electronic library: New roles for librarians. *Cause/Effect.* 20 (1), 45-51.

Rapple, B. A (1995). The librarian as teacher in the network environment. *College Teaching.* 45 (3), 114-116.

Rice-Lively, M. L. and J.D. Racine. (1997, January). The role of academic librarians in the era of inforation technology. *Journal of Academic Librarianship.* pp. 31-41.

St. Lifer, E. (1996). Net Work: New roles, same mission. *Library Journal.* 121 (19), 26-30.

Shifflett, L. (1996). Louis Shores: Defining Educational Librarianship. Maryland: Scarecrow Press.

Skiadas, C.H. (1999). The role of libraries in a changing academic environment. Greece: Technical University of Crete. ERIC: ED 433 837, 1-10, June, 1999.

Wilson, T. (1995). The role of the librarian in the 21st century. University of Sheffield. Keynote address for the Library Association Northern Branch Conference, Longhirst, Northumberland, November 17, 1995.

Shedding the Stereotypes:
Librarians in the 21st Century

Pixey Anne Mosley

SUMMARY. While it is very difficult to predict exactly what a librarian's job will entail in 50 years, there is no doubt in the author's mind that the profession will be a successful one. Exploring today's societal and technological trends allows one to propose an idea of patterns and expectations typical of the next generation of librarians and the challenges that come in managing this talented, yet demanding, group. *[Article copies available for a fee from The Haworth Document Delivery Service: 1-800-HAWORTH. E-mail address: <docdelivery@haworthpress.com> Website: <http://www. HaworthPress.com> © 2002 by The Haworth Press, Inc. All rights reserved.]*

KEYWORDS. Librarian stereotypes, transitions, role of technology, Generation X

Trying to gaze into a crystal ball and characterize the librarian of the future is impossible in this age of rapid change, shedding of stereotypes, and redirecting of services. Similarly, describing a day in the life of a typical professional reference librarian or cataloger over the next 25 years is a truly speculative activity. However, the exercise offers an opportunity to identify and open for discussion some issues that are criti-

Pixey Anne Mosley is Associate Professor, Director of Access Services, Evans Library, Texas A&M University, 5000 TAMU, College Sation, TX 77843-5000 (E-mail: pmosley@tamu.edu).

[Haworth co-indexing entry note]: "Shedding the Stereotypes: Librarians in the 21st Century." Mosley, Pixey Anne. Co-published simultaneously in *The Reference Librarian* (The Haworth Information Press, an imprint of The Haworth Press, Inc.) No. 78, 2002, pp. 167-176; and: *The Image and Role of the Librarian* (ed: Wendi Arant, and Candace R. Benefiel) The Haworth Information Press, an imprint of The Haworth Press, Inc., 2002, pp. 167-176. Single or multiple copies of this article are available for a fee from The Haworth Document Delivery Service [1-800-HAWORTH, 9:00 a.m. - 5:00 p.m. (EST). E-mail address: docdelivery@ haworthpress.com].

http://www.haworthpress.com/store/product.asp?sku=J120
© 2002 by The Haworth Press, Inc. All rights reserved.
10.1300/J120v37n78_11

cal to growth and development of our future colleagues and successors, as well as the library organization as a whole. One constant that can be established with some confidence is the increasing role of technology in the execution of daily tasks and as part of the interaction expectations of many users while still supporting some traditional roles and responsibilities. Finding the balance between technology and traditional service will be especially difficult given the wide variation in expectations and funding at different libraries.

Some doomsday predictors have suggested the forthcoming demise of the professional librarian due to obsolescence in the face of end user direct access to the Internet. If one should define a professional librarian as the traditional stereotype of the mousy, old-maid introvert who severely enforces library rules on silence, sends users to a small group of classic reference tools, and controls the access to collections with suspicion and punitive action, then the demise has already occurred and we shall all shout "Hurrah!" over it. Today's reference librarians bear very little resemblance to librarians of 75 years ago, both in appearance and specific job tasks and responsibilities. The fact that the changes have often been ongoing transitional ones with periodic dramatic high points, such as the introduction of a library's first electronic catalog or circulation system, tends to camouflage the truly extensive change that the profession has already undergone. Those who have remained as leaders in the profession can take a moment to reflect back and bear personal witness to the broad changes that have occurred during the past 25 years. There is no reason to expect that the profession would suddenly freeze in time and that next year's newly hired MLIS graduates will be replicas of the MLS graduates of 10 years ago. In fact, they will bring different experiences, education, and expectations to the professional environment. The future will not bring the demise for a profession as resilient and robust as librarianship; but it will challenge the ability to innovate and adapt to new expectations, communication styles, and tools.

DEFINING SOME CHALLENGES

The next few decades will continue to be ones of transition and role redefinition for librarians. Even as electronic resources expand and gain ascendancy as the most convenient format for many users, librarians will continue to have responsibilities in maintaining education and awareness among their user communities about an extensive body of recorded knowledge in paper and other archival formats, and in reaffirming that the recorded word does not begin and end with the Internet. It is not a glamorous role, reminding people that research can be challenging or tedious, but librarians in public and educational institutions have an ethical responsibility, from both a societal perspective and often as a peer to the academic teacher.

In addition to the reminders about print resources, there are many aspects of electronic resource access and information seeking that librarians will have to understand and explain to users, thereby undoing many advertising-based misconceptions. Though some publishers are working to provide retrospective digitization with good results, the associated financial costs and intellectual property issues blur marketing and political hype about the "free access for all to everything." Librarians will continue to encounter confusion over copyright limitations and try to explain the convoluted issues to users. As litigation is decided, with outcomes such as that of *Tasini v. New York Times*, publishers may encounter increasing difficulty in providing electronic access and availability of a considerable amount of 20th and early 21st century information. Similarly, there are literally millions of monographs that will never be converted to the electronic media because the interest is too limited for it to be successful as a commercial venture or it is not special/rare/ unique enough to warrant research grant-funding for library-based digitization, electronic storage, and distribution. This material must be kept available, and with as many access points and as much description as possible short of full-text digitization to enhance its appeal and perceived relevancy to users working in the "information on-demand" model.

Finally, librarians will continue to serve a very diverse spectrum of user needs in a variety of ways. From the traditional reference desk to the office consultation to the virtual reference interview, librarians will have to be adaptable to the communication skills of their users. For the young child, the academic student, the information-seeking adult, and the venerable emeritus faculty researcher, libraries and librarians have a potential role of ongoing interaction. The direction that they take in developing that potential will define the future of the profession. There are several hypothetical models with multiple variations. These models range from one of fast food information delivery addressing the specific, immediate content needs of the user to maintaining the traditional stereotypical archival model as keepers of the book mausoleum for serious researchers. In truth, the future will probably be one that merges and adapts parts of every model to a larger scope of service rather than a single narrow purpose and philosophy. If librarians and administrators want to play an active role in the future, they must work to develop a shared vision of the paths they wish to follow and take an active role in creating their destiny by reaching beyond the walls of the library and forming alliances with other educators or community groups. Reticence and vague traditionalism, retreating behind the cloak of "providing for the common good," or "protecting the collection" will only lead to being mothballed. There is no single or correct role for every librarian in every library. Rather there is the need to be clear-sighted, responsive, flexible and proactive with user interactions and the services being provided.

A SECOND TECHNOLOGY CAREER

Having discussed some of the challenging roles facing a hypothetical librarian of the future, one could ask whether the people populating the profession are up to such a difficult task. As with any profession, some librarians will be outstanding performers while others will be marginal. However, the potential to find the needed skillset and attitudes are there, if nurtured and embraced appropriately.

As this article is being written, the downsizing, failure, and rebirth of dot-com and other technology-based companies have become a regular news coverage issue, to the point of being parodied in the *Doonesbury* comic strips. Some of these, such as the 2001 *Chronicle of Higher Education* reports about the NetLibrary bankruptcy filing and subsequent purchase of assets by OCLC, and the extensive layoffs at Questia, have an identifiable and immediate impact on libraries and generate significant shockwaves throughout the professional psyche. As many library and information science graduates had been recruited into the technology sector during the past several years, these librarians may now rediscover one of the advantages of academic and civil service libraries: job security. For agile organizations ready to embrace this employee, it will serve to reintroduce and infuse into the traditional library environment, struggling to embrace technology, a new type of librarian. It is a librarian who may need retraining in traditional reference sources or cataloging procedures but who offers in return a high technology literacy level, individual flexibility, and multi-tasking expertise. Though not necessarily a subject specialist with specialized graduate education, the librarian may bring a knowledge-base or skill set that includes marketing techniques, customer service philosophy, innovative thinking, and positive teamwork expectations. Similarly, their exposure to the faster-paced corporate world will have provided them with the ability to learn new areas quickly and require shorter periods of orientation.

Supporting the economic impact issues, college placement centers are already reporting that they anticipate seeing a lower quantity of competing job offers coming to the next year or two of graduates in many disciplines. As reported in the *Chronicle of Higher Education* by Brownstein, the typically robust engineering and computer science areas are seeing reductions of 10% and 17% respectively and business bachelor's degrees are similarly affected. Even as early as March 2001 as reported by Vanscoy, analysts were predicting significant growth in versatile MBA programs. When there are fewer job opportunities in a chosen discipline where one already has developed expertise, non-thesis interdisciplinary graduate school programs, such as the MLIS or MBA, can begin looking more attractive. Library schools may be provided with an opportunity to capitalize on this and infuse the profession with contemporary subject expertise, balanced expectations, and enthusiasm for growth.

NEAR TERM GENERATIONAL ISSUES

As indicated by Stanley Wilder in "The Changing Profile of Research Library Professional Staff," the current core of the profession is an aging one that will see many retirements through the next decade. The number of librarians in the Generation X age group, born approximately in 1961-1981, are significantly lower than that found in comparable professions. This is the same group (20 to 40 year olds) that will be most affected by the economic issues mentioned above. However, the introduction and embracing of these new librarians into a traditional organizational environment may not be easy. Even as organizations desire to grow and develop new ideas, traditional management structures and professional organizations may need to take a deep breath and prepare to be flexible and patient as Generation X hits the library workplace in significant numbers.

Corporate environments have been working with Generation X for several years and have the literature to show it. Some of the most referenced books have been written and updated by authors such as William Strauss, Bruce Tulgan, and Claire Raines. Similarly, the business theory and human resources journals have been exploring the issues of Generation X adaptations. The librarian profession has acknowledged awareness of Generation X, but usually in the context of serving them as demanding users, not in a coworker relationship. A forward looking article that appeared in *Illinois Libraries* in 1998 discusses issues of Generation X librarians within the context of what they are looking for in a professional position, but does not offer answers for the challenges that come with trying to meet their expectations within a publicly funded bureaucracy or union-based environment, nor does it address the conflict that may arise with the inclusion of Generation X in the professional ranks.

Generation X librarians are likely to have behavior patterns, personality quirks, and expectations that are misunderstood by senior staff and could be badly mishandled in the traditional hierarchical library setting. They have grown up and gone through the educational arena when teamwork and quality assurance are the buzzwords, asking "why" was encouraged, and the basic slogan is "just do it." Often they perceive department or individual boundaries as something to be swept away or a roadblock to accomplishing a successful change. Raised in the age of television and information, they are frequent multi-taskers and seem to process ideas from concept to application faster. When one contrasts this to many library organizations where decisions are reached by either a slow consensus process or in a top down manner, where "we have always done it this way and it works fine" is considered a valid justification against operational change, it is easy to see where conflict arises over strategic expectations. Similarly, supervisors should be wary of making assumptions about anticipating or dictating how much time a task should take when assigning it to an enthusiastic Generation X librarian. In the business world, supervisors are finding that because Generation Xers were raised in an environment of visual learning, information overload, and multi-tasking neural development, they are able to make more efficient and effective use of their work time than their predecessors. For this reason it is extremely important to evaluate these employees in terms of task accomplishment rather than whether they "appear" to be working hard all the time. How an organization manages and balances these issues and conflicts could make a big difference in its being poised for future growth. Alienating Generation X librarians with pedantic rules and no opportunities for growth and creativity will contribute to an organization fading away like a dinosaur. Instead managers will be challenged to direct their enthusiasm and lack of bureaucratic patience in a direction consistent with overall organizational objectives, and nurture a staff blending and knowledge sharing based on mutual respect and shared vision.

In addition to organizational bureaucracy and misunderstood initiative, another potential area of conflict may be one of perceived job value and work ethic differences. Unlike prior generations, Generation Xers do not invest as much of their personal self-worth, identity, and time into their jobs. They work hard but do not follow the philosophies of prior generations that define them as individuals based primarily on their employment status and longevity. Generation X has grown up in the transitory society of cross-country relocations and corporate layoffs and do not expect to work for the same employer for 25 years. Many pursue non-bookish hobbies and interests outside of the workplace. A recent article by Fountain in the *New York Times* brought attention to the changing image of librarians as people who describe themselves as "adventurous" and "popular culture junkie," and have hobbies that include surfing, yoga, jazz, and in-line skating. Their commitment to their lives outside of work may have significant impact on managers in library environments where there are perceptual expectations of significant overtime or volunteering for night/weekend shifts or working on academic tenure requirements outside of the normal work schedule. Telling a potential Generation X librarian that they will be expected to put in a 50+ hour week on a regular basis and will be at the bottom of the list for leave requests or schedule flexibility their first 5 years will almost always result in their self-eliminating from the pool of candidates and turning down the offer. Just because they may be coming to traditional library settings due to economic downturns in the private sector, does not correlate to their having an attitude of a desperate beggar that will meekly accept what they perceive as unrealistic and unreasonable expectations. As put forth by Strauss and Tulgan, the average Generation X employee is not seeking anything too different from prior generations—respect, a voice, etc. The difference is that they will walk away if an employer or organization does not live up to their expectations. To put it bluntly, they are flexible and adaptable enough to live without us, but we cannot live without them.

Finally, with the profession breaking out of the stereotype and having more emphasis on lifestyle issues, the need for disposable, luxury income is increased. Librarians of the future are going to want higher salaries. According to articles by Kalan and Farley in *American Libraries*, some librarian salaries are too low and there are hints for a profession-wide movement addressing this. Even librarians who have been forced out of the high pay, generous benefits dot-com environments do not consider poverty-level salary acceptable. Combined with the graduate academic requirements and the increasingly versatile job responsibilities, librarians are going to demand higher salaries and more solid benefits, along with the workplace issues addressed previously.

In some ways, academic library managers and librarians are in a position to be less shocked by the workplace introduction of Generation X as colleagues than the corporate business world. Being a service-based profession to the young, they have already taken a first look at working with the next generation as shelving or clerical student workers. Looking at the academic freshmen with their idealism, naïve expectations, and assertive activism is looking at the Generation Y that will be joining the profession in a few years. The trap many fall into is to label deep generational differences as immaturity or impetuous youthfulness when, in fact, the basic generational identity has already been formed. Other tensions may be eased by the fact that front line service librarians and librarians turned managers are less likely to be locked into their age designated generational mold. Many may have already picked up some of the Generation X and Y mannerisms, sayings, or philosophies and are likely to be more tolerant of youthful expression from encountering it on a daily basis.

In addition to bringing new ideas, perspectives, energy, enthusiasm, and intelligence, Generation X librarians will be a needed link to understanding and providing effective service to the next groups of users (and eventual colleagues), Generation Y/Nexters and Generation D (for digital; the tentative term being coined in advertising). With each generation, there are new differences and challenges, but they occur in a progressive way, oftentimes in reaction to the immediately preceding generation. Gaining a better understanding of Generation X motivation and learning to accept them will better prepare an organization for embracing Generation Y.

OTHER PROFESSION CHANGES

One objective that has been adopted at numerous levels in the profession and its supporting organizations is diversity. As library school recruitment programs expand to more students with non-traditional backgrounds and libraries themselves encourage positive interactions on race and ethnicity issues, the profession will move in this direction. One positive effect of infusing the profession with Generation X, Generation Y, and Generation D may be to introduce more tolerance and acceptance of diversity initiatives to enable the profession to better reflect the population ethnicity demographics in the U.S. According to Raines, the Generation Xers are considerably more comfortable with diversity issues than previous generations.

Another change already starting to show up in the business sector is the concept of employment as a function of place. In parallel to the expectations of many users for information needs to be met remotely using technology, it may be that many librarians can do their jobs without having to be in an office in the library or sitting at a physical reference desk. Granted it is pretty hard to shelve books remotely, but many tasks of the professional librarian are moving into a format that could allow someone with a sophisticated computer workstation at home (and the blessing and cooperation of their administration) to complete many tasks without coming into the building. The pre-order tools of collection development, publisher catalogs, approval plan forms via email, and the library's holdings catalog have all moved into an electronic environment. Other positions, such as an electronic resources cataloger or virtual reference (chat) librarian are heavily oriented to the telecommuting environment. A position and justification of a defined organizational philosophy on this issue may become more critical as technology demands and those comfortable with the concepts infuse the profession.

CONCLUSION

This article identifies several areas of the profession that will need to adapt to changing expectations. Even as librarians grow and make an effort to stay current in the rapidly changing global technology environment, they will always be faced with the challenge of simultaneous learning, implementation, and planning. The issues of tomorrow will always seem to be more complex than the current ones. In terms of peers and colleagues, the next generation will always seem to have a frustratingly high comfort level with the latest and greatest technology and a set of job expectations that feel slightly discordant and demanding. By embracing these librarians into the profession and working to meet the challenges proactively, an ongoing chain will be forged that ties the value of information to the users of library services, be they children, academic students and faculty, or a retired senior citizen.

REFERENCES

Bradford, Lawrence J., Claire Raines, and Jo Leda Martin. *Twentysomething: Managing and Motivating Today's New Workforce.* New York: MasterMedia Ltd., 1992.
Brownstein, Andrew. "Enrollment Shifts and Last-Minute Aid Requests Signal the Onset of an Economic Downturn," *Chronicle of Higher Education* 20 April 2001;

available electronically at <http://chronicle.com> Section: Special Report (accessed 30 November 2001).

Carlson, Scott. "A Company That Offers an Online Library Lays Off Half Its Employees," *Chronicle of Higher Education* 29 November 2001; available electronically at <http://chronicle.com> Section: Information Technology (accessed 30 November 2001).

Cooper, Julie F. and Cooper, Eric A. "Generational Dynamics and Librarianship: Managing Generation X," *Illinois Libraries* 80, no.1 (1998): 18-21.

Farley, Yvonne Snyder. "Strategies for Improving Library Salaries," *American Libraries* 33, no.1 (February 2002): 56-59.

Fountain, John W. "Librarians Adjust Image to Fill Jobs," *New York Times*, 23 August 2001; available from *Lexis/Nexis Academic Universe*, <http://web.lexis-nexis.com/universe> (accessed 23 August 2001).

Kalan, Abby. "There is No Honor in Being Underpaid," *American Libraries* 33, no.1 (February 2002): 52–54.

Mulhauser, Dana. "New College Graduates Face Tight Job Market, Survey Finds," *Chronicle of Higher Education* 29 November 2001; available electronically at <http://chronicle.com> Section: Today's News (accessed 30 November 2001).

Raines, Claire. *Beyond Generation X: A Practical Guide for Managers.* Menlo Park, CA: Crisp Publications, 1997.

Strauss, William and Neil Howe. *Generations: History of America's Future, 1584 to 2069.* New York: William Morrow & Company, Inc., 1991.

Trudeau, Garry. *Doonesbury*, myVulture storyline, July 2, 2001-July 6, 2001; available electronically at <http://www.doonesbury.com/strip/dailydose/index.htm> (accessed 29 November 2001).

Tulgan, Bruce. *Managing Generation X: How to Bring Out the Best in Young Talent.* revised and updated ed. New York: WW Norton & Company, 2000.

Vanscoy, Holly. "Riding Out the Recession," *Ziff Davis Smart Business for the New Economy* 14, no. 3 (March 2001): 34.

Wilder, Stanley. "The Changing Profile of Research Library Professional Staff," *ARL: A Bimonthly Report on Research Library Issues and Actions from ARL, CNI, and SPARC*, Association of Research Libraries, 208/209 (Feb/Apr 2000): 1-5.

Young, Jeffrey R. "netLibrary Files for Bankruptcy Protection," *Chronicle of Higher Education* 30 November 2001; available electronically at <http://chronicle.com> Section: Information Technology (accessed 30 November 2001).

Young, Jeffrey R. "NetLibrary Files for Bankruptcy Protection, and OCLC Offers to Buy Its Assets," *Chronicle of Higher Education* 16 November 2001; available electronically at <http://chronicle.com> Section: Information Technology (accessed 30 November 2001).

Young, Jeffrey R. "E-Book Provider netLibrary Puts Itself Up for Sale, Worrying Librarians," *Chronicle of Higher Education*, 18 October 2001; available electronically at <http://chronicle.com> Section: Information Technology (accessed 30 November 2001).

Zemke, Ron, Claire Raines, and Bob Filipczak. *Generations at Work: Managing the Clash of Veterans, Boomers, Xers, and Nexters in Your Workplace.* Atlanta, GA: AMACOM: American Management Association, 2000.

Index

Page numbers followed by t indicate tables.

http://www.haworthpress.com/store/product.asp?sku=J120
© 2002 by The Haworth Press, Inc. All rights reserved.
10.1300/J120v37n78_12